Longmans' sociology of education

The sociology of the school

In this study the school is examined as a social
organisation in its own right. The structure and
functions of both primary and secondary
schools are analysed using the language, concepts and models of sociology in a way designed
to introduce students not only to a fresh view
of their own experience, but also to a fresh
approach, through sociology, to problems in
education.

After an introduction relating schools to
society as a whole, structural–functional and
conflict models of the school are studied. Finally,
attention is given to organizational aspects of
the school. The list of books for further reading
has been carefully compiled to meet the needs
of students entirely new to sociology as well as
the requirements of those intending to study the
subject in depth.

Longmans' sociology of education

The sociology of the school

M D Shipman
Worcester College of Education

Humanities Press
New York

First published in the United States of America 1968
by Humanities Press Inc

© *M. D. Shipman 1968*

First published 1968

Printed in Great Britain by
Cox & Wyman Ltd
London, Fakenham and Reading

Contents

Contents

Preface

In the rapid development of interest in the sociology of education in Britain, attention has been concentrated on the relation between social inequality and education. This has stemmed from the interest of sociologists in social class, as a most marked feature of British society. The content of courses, research projects and the subject matter of textbooks, reflect this priority. The result has been a picture of the school as an arena where the objectives of education are frustrated by the influence of neighbourhood, family, peer group, social class and occupation. The school has rarely been studied as a social organization of interest in its own right, although often as a centre of conflicting external pressures. This book attempts such a study.

There are two main objectives:
1. To give a description of primary and secondary schools as social organizations, with their own culture and group life.
2. To introduce some of the language, concepts and models of sociology while analysing the working of schools.

These two combined give a sociological perspective of the school. The research on which the book is based has been drawn from many disciplines. The sociological language has been simplified and the models pruned of many accessories. Yet the hope is that the perspective remains that of a sociologist, and that the reader will catch some of the excitement that this can bring when it is used on a familiar organization.

Many colleagues at the Worcester College of Education helped in the preparation of this book. Miss B. Sheridan advised on infant schools and corrected many of my mistakes in this field. Helpful criticisms and advice were given by Mrs E. Wormald, Mr M. Bowker and Mr W. Edwards. Mr P. Hÿtch not only advised on the junior school, but gave continuous guidance at all stages. Mrs Margaret Shipman helped prepare the final draft and helped throughout to keep the work firmly anchored in the school situation. All will find their own insights in the book.

Acknowledgements

We are indebted to the following for permission to reproduce copyright material:

H.M. Stationery Office for quotations from 'Half Our Future' in the *Newsom Report*; W. W. Norton & Co. Incorporated for an extract from *Psychoanalysis of Group Behavior* by Scheidlinger; National Foundation For Educational Research In England & Wales for tables from *A Survey of Reward and Punishments in Schools* by Highfield and Pinsent; Routledge & Kegan Paul Ltd for extracts from *The Teacher's Role* by B. Wilson; and John Wiley & Sons Ltd for extracts from *Sociology of Teaching* by Waller.

Part I

Introduction

1

School in society

Education is the organized part of the process through which each successive generation learns the accumulated knowledge of a society. This cultural transmission is necessary so that people can fit into the existing pattern of life and associate with others in a predictable, efficient and humane way. The baby is converted into a social being by his parents and near kin. However haphazard this action, the achievements are complex, particularly the learning of language. After this initial training, societies differ in the organization of further learning, not only in the content and length of education but in the agencies involved.

The involvement of education in the process of converting children into useful, responsible adults means that it is never concerned solely with knowledge as preparation for occupation. Inevitably it has to ensure that each generation shares a common set of values, the same ideas of right and wrong. This moral education must be accompanied by social training in appropriate behaviour. Its objective is a disciplined as well as an informed adult. Inevitably this has involved religious teaching, for this reinforces and sanctions social training.

Preparation for, and regulation of, social life determines the content of education. Schools are agencies of socialization operating alongside the family, religion, the social services and the local community. In a complex society there is no guarantee that these will share common values, and pupils and staff may experience conflict as they play their parts in each of them.

Because schools are frequently trying to transmit values which are not shared by the other influences on their pupils, they work against, as well as with, other agencies of socialization. In order to exclude adverse influences opposed to the paramount values which it supports, a school must approximate to a hot-house. Staff must try to organize the school as a model of what life should be, moral, disciplined, hard-working and friendly.

Unfortunately, the more deviant the area which a school serves, the greater will be the contrast between its values and those of the school. The teachers, mainly from middle-class backgrounds, meet children whose beliefs and behaviour are rooted in very different environments. The result is frequently the frustration of the teachers and a rejection of school by the children. Consequently the influence of the school is smallest on just those children who could benefit most.

Such conflict is less likely in small-scale, simple societies. Here, religion, occupation, family and community life, law and politics are pervaded by the same values, and the young are liable to be continually exposed to reinforcing adult influences. In these circumstances schools for organized learning are often superfluous. Nevertheless, the preparation of the young is not left to chance.[1] Even where there is no apparent attempt at formal training, a child is guided and stimulated to observe and copy adult behaviour. All the experiences are meaningful because they are a model of what his life will be and at all times this relevance is clear. The child can see his own future in the lives of adults around him. This ceases when change becomes normal and the range of opportunities increases.

However, most preliterate societies test that the male child has acquired the skills and values necessary for him to play a full part as an adult, before giving him this status. Around puberty there is usually tuition to ensure that a child is ready for initiation. This is accompanied by elaborate ritual and intensive instruction in the history and religious secrets of the group by the elders. Frequently there is a further testing of physical, mental and moral readiness at this time. Girls are given a less extensive initiation and are usually prepared for marriage and household management.

In many African tribes this teaching took place in schools. These were built specially for this purpose, away from the village, and the novices lived there until ready for initiation. The stay varied from a few months to several years. Some schools were permanent, with successive intakes, while others were built specially for one age group. Boys were taught by selected teachers to fight in a disciplined manner, herd cattle, do a variety of crafts and to perform dances, songs, stories and religious rituals. Conditions were usually harsh and there were tests of proficiency before return into the adult life of the community.[2]

The stress in this schooling is on moral education and social training rather than preparation for occupation, which can be learnt informally.[3] It is backed by the full force of religion. Successful completion is usually marked symbolically by feasting, granting privileges and often bodily marking. Initiation transforms the child into an adult with all the rights and obligations implied. It is often, however, merely an introduction to the mysteries of the sacred life, full knowledge being granted only to the elders.

With few exceptions, such societies have evolved into larger, more complex forms. The complexity is essentially an increased division of labour whereby each person plays different roles in many different institutions. Each of these roles tends to be one part in the whole organization and involves learning only part of the total culture. A welder in a car assembly plant knows little of the other skills employed in making a car or of the working of the management. In small-scale societies near subsistence level, each man must know all the technical and social skills to enable him to approach self-sufficiency within his family. In modern societies, men work, worship and take their leisure in large-scale organizations of which only a small part is visible to the participant. Further, each organization may demand different types of behaviour. There has been structural differentiation in such fields as government, administration, communication, religion and social welfare, and this has also produced the school as we know it. There has also been a break-up of the cultural unity of simple societies, so that each of these specialist organizations tends to develop its own values, not necessarily identical with the rest. Thus the values stressed in school may conflict with those in work or church.

Advanced industrial societies also change fast. Parents or kin can no longer prepare the next generation for their occupations because they will be doing different jobs, using different skills, in different places. Schools and colleges take over this preparation. They find it difficult to adapt fast enough and are frequently teaching for a world that has passed by. But they give each child opportunities that parents cannot offer in staffing and equipment, and they still give a moral education whose object is continuity rather than change, regulation rather than innovation. They still teach the social behaviour expected of adults in certain positions. In a rapidly changing world, this too leads to friction between the school and other agencies in the society.

The successive phases of structural differentiation affect schools as they affect any other organization. The elementary, all-age school splits up into infant, junior and secondary. The secondary stage divides into grammar, technical and modern schools or streams. Higher education branches into universities, advanced technological and research institutions, specialist colleges of education and art, and a number of technical colleges with different functions. Within each school and college teaching becomes more specialized, starting with higher education and spreading through secondary levels until the general subjects teacher becomes a rarity above the primary level. With each new structural division there is the accompanying problem of a weakening in consensus over values. Not only are educational values liable to clash with those outside, but within each school, specialization creates its own stresses.

These changes have meant that schools are involved in another function alongside preparation and regulation, for the young must be allocated to occupations and this is no longer determined at birth, once large-scale organization replaces family and patronage. Education becomes progressively more important in deciding adult status and is consequently involved in political and social arguments over equality of opportunity. This is concerned more with access to education than its content. Inside the school, teaching is building up new ways of thinking and behaving, appropriate to the positions that pupils will occupy, which are frequently different from those experienced in the homes from which they come. M. Mead has written that 'Modern education includes a heavy emphasis upon the function of education to create discontinuities – to turn the child of the peasant into a clerk, of the farmer into a lawyer, of the Italian immigrant into an American, of the illiterate into the literate'.[4] But after the conversion into an industrial, urban society has been accomplished, the process must continue. This is illustrated by the following passage from M. Herkovits:[5]

The homogeneity of the [Zuni] culture makes for a unity of cultural aims and methods of inculcating them in the young, and thus leaves little room for conflict between the directives given by different preceptors. . . . This conflict in directives is perhaps the source of the most serious difficulties in larger, less homogeneous societies, where the total educational process includes schooling as well as training in the home. Serious conflicts may result from education received at the hand of persons whose cultural or sub-cultural frames of reference differ.

In contemporary industrial societies, rapid technical and social change creates a persistent conflict, not only between social classes with different values, but between groups in the van and rear of these changes. As schools become a major agent of cultural transmission they are placed in the centre of this controversy over values. Some people will try to use schools as agencies for producing radical, technically efficient and forward-looking citizens. But some will try to use them to delay the change to new styles of life and thought.

Industrial societies are also socially mobile, as children decreasingly follow their parents' occupations. The grammar school in Britain today is an agency which can provide the means for a working class child to move up the social ladder. Inevitably some parents and some children will refuse to accept its values in order to avoid alienation from family and friends. Whatever the pattern of education, it will be involved in promoting and demoting, with all the tensions this involves for children and their parents.

The arrival of schools is therefore one part of an increase in specialization in society. Today we have an education system that sorts children into a variety of paths along which they will receive educations of different lengths and content. All children start in a primary school, but they finish in all manner of secondary schools or institutions of higher education.

The growth of a school system

In an historically short period the school has become a vital agency in the preparation of all children for their adult roles in industrial societies. In the schools examined by anthropologists in Africa, the emphasis was on military training, ensuring discipline, preserving tribal traditions and religious ritual. But the Western pattern has been different, for here the object has been more vocational. While schools have been founded for a variety of reasons and purposes, they originally tended to provide the priests and administrators required as the scale and complexity of social life increased. Wherever religion and administration depended on writing, a corps of literate men was required. Further, powerful religions coincided with empires that needed good, written communications.

The first schools recorded in history were in the ancient civilizations of Babylon, Egypt and China between 2000 and 3000 B.C. These were the first known complex societies, using improved farming techniques on fertile soil to produce a surplus of food for courts, towns and non-productive priests, soldiers and administrators. These were the first societies known to rely on written communications and their schools produced a small number of literate bureaucrats, mainly priests.

The Western tradition of education developed from this. It was concerned only with a minority until very recently, for few were needed to govern. It was organized by the Church, which employed the majority of the literate. It was primarily interested in teaching the classical languages and culture that enabled this minority to communicate and hand down their learning. It was concentrated in urban, religious centres where there was the wealth to support schools and scope for the educated man.

Industrialization, and the movement into towns that accompanied it, created a need for widespread education. The new urban, industrial family was outside the close social control exerted in the older village life. The debate over the desirability of extending education was between those who saw it as a threat to the docility and industry of the masses, and those who saw it as a means to these ends. As industrial, urban life became complex and the demand for technical and clerical skills grew, education had to expand. This demand has continued to grow and has dominated education in the twentieth century. Finally, education slowly became the main avenue to a good job. In the last hundred years, the new professions which have grown fast have been entered by examination, while academic success has come to mean more than family background in the older professions such as law and medicine. This has brought the schools into the spotlight of the debate over equality of opportunity.

The growth and specialization of schools was, therefore, a response to social needs. The form which education took was influenced by the educationists, but within the limits set by the existing social framework. Frequently the ideas of pioneers have only been influential after their death, once social conditions have changed in a direction which has made them relevant. The charity schools of the eighteenth century, the monitorial system of the early nineteenth, and payment by results after 1861 reflected the conditions of their time, not the hopes of the philosophers. These had to wait until education became an economic necessity in a richer society that had no need for child labour and could afford to keep children in school longer.

The curriculum and teaching methods have also reflected the social climate. Until well into the nineteenth century, reading and writing took second place to religious and moral training in the effort to civilize the new urban masses. The catechetical question and answer technique mirrored the certainty of adults in their authority and knowledge. Only when social conditions had improved and scientific, sceptical inquiry became necessary in the more complex, changing world of the last hundred years, did the existing curriculum and child-centred approach take shape.

The school in industrial society

The transformation of economic and social life has proceeded far enough for the skills and discipline of urban life to become part of our culture. Mid twentieth-century Britain has established urban, industrial values which dominate country as well as town. Under these conditions, schools have to satisfy new social and economic needs. Many of the strains dealt with in later chapters arise in the course of adaptation to these.

An industrial, urban society has the following characteristics:

1. Rapidly changing productive techniques, requiring an advanced division of labour in large-scale organizations.
2. A class and prestige structure, resulting from the new relationships between occupations, accompanied by a new distribution of power.
3. Values which are increasingly rational and materialistic.
4. An acceptance of change as normal.

Each of these influences the schools which are a vital part of this industrial system.

1. *Economic influences*

An increasingly complicated technology must be run by a highly skilled labour force. It is accompanied by administration, government and communication demanding professional and clerical skills. There must be, therefore, a progressive extension of education. The Newcastle Commission reported in 1861 that only 5·4 per cent remained in school beyond thirteen, the large majority having left before the age of eleven.[6] Within a hundred years, secondary education has been provided for all and the need for talent to be utilized has necessitated a rapid increase of students doing advanced work in universities and colleges in various branches of higher education. This expansion is universal and increasing. The Robbins Report on Higher Education stated in 1963 that 'About everywhere we have travelled we have been impressed by an urge to educational development, and a valuation of the importance of higher education, which has often been translated into plans for expansion far surpassing the scale of present British plans.'[7] But there is also a need to raise standards for all, as new technology requires higher proportions of skilled men.

This increased demand for skills applies at all levels. The farm labourer as well as the industrial worker uses machines of great complexity. The office as well as the factory tends to become larger

and more complicated. Technology also eases the job of the house-
wife, provided she has the skill to operate the apparatus. Behind
these changes are a growing number of professional, technical and
scientific workers. The fastest growth in employment is in those
occupations requiring a long education. The lack of skilled men has
been a continuous obstacle to economic growth and the Industrial Training Act of 1964 and the expansion of education at
all levels have been designed to rectify this shortage. The foreseeable
ends of this trend are the automated factory and office, with their
maintenance men and technologists, but with few operatives or
clerks.

This need to utilize available talent in advanced industrial economies has been an important factor in focusing attention on the
problem of those who have not, so far, benefited from education. In
England and Wales, the Newsom and Plowden Committees have
both recommended special financial help for education in problem
areas. In America, several ambitious schemes are in operation.[8] The
Higher Horizons programme in New York was started in 1956: by
1960 it covered sixty-three elementary and junior high schools.
Talented children, mainly Negroes or Puerto Ricans, were selected
for special courses to raise their academic achievements and aspirations. Special staff and funds were allocated to bring them up to a
level where they could enter college, while simultaneously giving
them experience of the advantages of higher education as a motivation. This programme has acted as a model for a number of city
and state projects such as the Ford Foundation's Great Cities Grey
Areas Programme.

To give under-privileged children a chance of benefiting from
their education, Project Head Start was inaugurated in 1965 as part
of the 'War on Poverty' of the Office of Economic Opportunity. This
provides children of three to five years old with the medical, cultural
and educational help they need, so that they will have more chance
of keeping up with the more privileged once they enter school. In
the summer of 1965, 561,359 children in 2,398 communities were
involved in the programme. In 1966, 125,000 children were also
involved in a year-round programme, in addition to the one of eight
weeks in the summer. The Head Start budget in 1966 was 180

million dollars. This operation relied on local community effort financed by the Office of Economic Opportunity. In many ways it is similar to the literacy campaigns that have been carried out in developing countries.

Head Start, as with any preschool programme, depends on the schools themselves being adequate in the deprived areas. The Elementary and Secondary Education Act of 1965 in America allocated over 1,000 million dollars to help local school districts broaden and strengthen public school programmes where there were concentrations of under-privileged children.

America faces problems of technological unemployment, immigrant and migrant groups, isolated and depressed regions that are far more severe than in Britain. Efforts to face these problems illustrate the concern of wealthy societies for their less fortunate members. While it has been argued that this is sound economic sense and a safeguard against possible social disorder, it also indicates a change in attitude towards equality of opportunity. As education becomes more important as a determinant of adult status, efforts are made to ensure that no one has too gross a handicap. An advanced economy rests on its education system and in turn provides the means for spreading education through all social levels and lengthening its duration.

These economic trends are summed up by P. Drucker in *Landmarks of Tomorrow* as follows:[9]

What has happened is a sudden, sharp change in the meaning and impact of knowledge for society. Because we can now organize men of high skill and knowledge, that is highly educated men, for joint work through the exercise of responsible judgement, the highly educated man has become the central resource of today's society, the supply of such men the true measure of its economic, its military and even its political potential.

From being a luxury on the periphery of social life, the school has become a crucial influence. Advanced economies rest on an educated society.

2. Social relations

New methods of production involve new relationships in working and social life. New occupational groups emerge, until the largest classes have become the industrial worker and the salaried middle class. But there is no clearly defined or legally sanctioned boundary between them. Movement from one to another is possible, and ability is theoretically the basis for allocation.

These new social classes, based on industrial processes, have developed their own associations for negotiating at work, their own values and their own means of exerting power. The 1832 Reform Act was the first signal of the steady takeover of political power by the middle class, and this was later balanced by the emergence of the Labour Party from the Trade Union movement. These adjust their philosophies and policies according to the economic and social aspirations of their potential supporters.

In a mobile society, an individual's personal ambitions, or his aspirations for his children, are unlimited. They are concentrated on the means available for fulfilment. In the early phases of industrialization, with small competitive firms employing simple machines, capital, however modest, was the prerequisite of success. As the organizations get larger and must use costly machines and offices, the era of the self-made man passes. In advanced industrial societies education becomes the main determinant of adult status. A minority still enjoy wealth, power and prestige through inheritance, but this too must increasingly be used to buy a good education, if the power is to be exercised.

Consequently the school is not only crucially placed because it satisfies the need of the economy for a skilled working force. It has become the agency fulfilling or frustrating individual ambitions. Allocation to a particular school or to a particular class within it, the quality of teaching and the response to it, the strength of motivation determining the use made of ability, all help to determine not only attainment in school, but position in adult life.

Schools have been affected by this, probably without many teachers realizing why their actions have been subjected to so much analysis by social scientists, and so much scrutiny by parents. But in marking work, assessing personality, streaming, setting and selection they are determining the whole future of the child, not only his success in school. The major debates on education since the war have, therefore, been on those aspects: the eleven-plus examination, intelligence testing, selection, the availability of external examinations in secondary schools, the proportion of grammar school and university places, the provision of comprehensive schools, which bear directly on this relation between education and occupation.

This has been described by Helmut Schelsky as follows:[10] 'In such a society, school easily becomes a kind of distributive agency conferring future social security, status, and consumption possibilities.' He sees two consequences of this. First, the parents cannot appraise the functions of the schools from a primarily educational point of view. Their first concern is whether the school is qualifying their child for a good job. Secondly, parents do not just demand the opportunity for their children to rise to a good position, they tend to claim such a position as a right. The teacher may be subject, therefore, to impossible demands, being required to ensure success regardless of ability, and having his ability as a teacher criticized on non-educational grounds.

The school, while at the centre of industrial society, is consequently subject to intense social pressures. It has become the agency for allocating individuals to their position in life and this inevitably involves demotion as well as promotion. The relation between these largely depends on the opportunities available, but this is determined by the economy, not the schools. Schools, however, have often avoided having to prepare for downward social movement, by preparing their pupils for positions of high prestige rather than those in short supply, for prestige tends to remain attached to some occupations long after their economic value has declined. The shortage of technicians, mathematicians and scientists is partly due to the lag in according them prestige.

These changes in the position of the school in society do not replace its function as an agency of socialization and social control. Indeed there are features of industrial society which require new social skills. The individual is no longer confined within a limited group of family and friends while he works or takes his leisure. It has been shown that schools are one aspect of the structural differentiation which marks the transition from an agricultural to an industrial society. As these specialist structures such as social ser-

vices, government offices, mass media, factories and offices pro-
liferate, individuals must learn to play roles in them. The appropriate
behaviour is very different from that sufficient in small, intimate
groups and cannot be learnt in the family. The school gives the
child his first experience of such behaviour, and also provides formal
preparation. The child learns to be one of a team, to be of service to
the school and his fellows; he also learns to channel his personality
and act on occasions as pupil, monitor, prefect, scientist, mathe-
matician, historian and so on. The school teaches him how to behave
unemotionally, to accept impartial assessment of his ability and
to base his behaviour on principles and rules. He is prepared for
participation in increasingly bureaucratic organizations.

A society of large organizations does not only demand a particular
type of behaviour, it also widens the choices open to the individual.
There is a greater variety of jobs, of diets, of means to financial
security, of partners, of areas to live in. Above all, mass production,
mass communication and good transport widen the range of choice
in consumption. Again the school provides experience of this and
helps provide a basis. As schools get larger and use methods in which
the child is active, more choices are forced on the pupils. Simultaneously there is a movement to make the final years in school a
help in settling into a world of often bewildering opportunities and
a preparation for increased leisure. The Newsom Report states:

The school can see that they have factual information for immediate
needs, and some clues as to where to turn for it in the future, in connection with employment, further education, and personal interests. And it
can begin to enlarge their understanding of the wider world, so that as
adults they may take a more satisfying part in it. As we see it, the school
programme, in the last year especially, ought to be deliberately out-
going.[11]

3. *Values*

The emergence of a new way of life involves new values. Implicit
in the concern over the way the schools determine the opportunities
of individuals are values held by those in the debate. The educational
issues of testing, streaming, selection and comprehensive education

have been complicated by the debate over equality among men. But schools, the agencies for preserving and handing on culture, tend to reflect the paramount values of the society they serve. An industrial society develops its own values, although these are frequently opposed by residues from the non-industrial past. Thus the English tradition of education has been deeply influenced by religion, and schools have the common act of worship that symbolizes their Christian purpose. There may be a trend towards secularization in society, but schools try to preserve the older values.

All industrial societies, whether Communist or capitalist, have in common a belief in the superiority of rational, scientific thought in dealing with material things. Industrial economies and urban life are triumphs of the use of reason to increase productivity and control environment. Belief in the supernatural or the traditional is progressively eliminated. It is replaced by a belief in the ability of rational-technical means to ensure material progress. This is part of the motivation necessary in contemporary economic life. There must be commitment to values which will produce efficient working. In Western industrial societies this is an individualistic ethic based on personal achievement, changing at the Communist end of the industrial spectrum into a collectivist ideal.

The school reflects this in its curriculum and teaching methods. The eighteenth-century school taught mainly Latin and a little Greek by methods of rote learning of a catechism, reinforced by the birch. The exceptions were the Non-Conformist academies, significantly the schools of many pioneers of the industrial revolution. The dramatic change came in the last quarter of the nineteenth century when a Royal Commission on scientific education reported from 1870 to 1875 and another on technical education in 1882 and 1884. From this time on, the classical tradition has been on the defensive.[12]

Another feature of this shift in values has been to question each item on the syllabus, asking the questions 'Does it serve a useful purpose?' 'What priority should it have?' and 'How should it be taught?' Thus the values behind the spread of science and technology also encourage research into the content and process of education.

This stress on challenging assumptions, on the value of research, on the efficiency and power of individual reason, also demolishes the traditional authority of teachers as carriers of accumulated wisdom and representatives of established order. Teachers have suffered a displacement similar to the priest, the magistrate and other agents of social control. B. Wilson has also pointed to characteristics in the teacher's role which complicate their position.[13] The broad, diffuse demands made on them as persons and the need to build up close affective relations with pupils, make the exercise of authority more difficult than in other professions, where relationships are neutral and skills specialist. Further, every adult has been through school and sees teaching and teachers in the light of this experience. The lawyer, doctor and solicitor are not exposed in this way.

Changes in the methods and content of education, the changing basis of authority of the teacher and the changing organization of schools are the results of the same change in values. The progressive school, motivating its pupils to learn actively, continually revising its curriculum, relying on informal, democratic means of control, reflects a society in which such values have become paramount. Where more traditional methods persist there is inevitably stress between the school and the society, and this manifests itself in the attitude of the pupils. In a period of change schools are inevitably poised between the necessity of preparing children for the new and preserving what is valued from the past.

4. *The normality of change*

The small-scale, simple societies which persisted for thousands of years, experienced very slow rates of change. Each generation would anticipate a similar life to those preceding it. From the eighteenth century in Britain this certainty was replaced by the realization that life was changing. This has more recently been replaced by a deliberate acceleration of the rate of change, through control over the scientific and technological processes which lie at the base of society. This is most marked in the increasing investment in research by industry, university and government. Most of this effort is directed towards improving productive techniques and methods of administration, but is extending to social research. The impetus comes from the demand for improved living standards and from economic and military competition between nations, but the effect is felt in all sectors of social life.

This rapid change associated with industrialization, and its stimulation by research, moves education from the periphery to the centre of the economy. The more complex a technology becomes, the more research is needed to sustain its development, and the more vital are schools and colleges. A school is now judged not only for its contribution to moral and social stability, but as an instrument in providing the right skills for a complex set of occupations. Further, it must produce students orientated towards sustaining the rate of change through an interest in research, and a population able to accommodate to the strains produced by change.

This emphasis affects the schools in two ways. First, it means that the curriculum must be subject to continual revision. Secondly, it disturbs the traditional relationships between teacher and pupil. Between the establishment of a school at Canterbury as an adjunct of the Cathedral in the sixth century and the end of the eighteenth century, there was little change in purpose. Education served to prepare clergy, particularly by teaching them Latin. The religious purpose had remained paramount through thirteen centuries. In the nineteenth century the school changed, as did all organizations, as an urban, industrial society developed.

The trend has been not only to replace the classics by subjects seen as more relevant to the modern world, but to replace the immutable by the changing. The frontiers of knowledge in science, mathematics, social studies and the technologies are continually expanding. Consequently, continual revision is necessary to ensure that syllabuses remain relevant. At the same time, the content and methods of traditional subjects have come increasingly under review. Curriculum studies, projects and experiments under the auspices of such bodies as the Schools Council and the Nuffield Foundation, are challenging existing practices.

Rapid change also affects the relation between pupil and teacher, already affected by the changed nature of the latter's authority. The schoolmaster of two hundred years ago was preparing his pupils to live in the same world in which he had grown up. They would use the same tools, share the same values, stay in the same place, have similar horizons. The teaching was dogmatic. A typical book for teachers was *The Preceptor's Assistant* by the Rev. D. Williams, published in 1819.[14] This 'progressive catechism of useful and necessary knowledge' consists of 250 pages of questions, with brief yet certain answers which the pupils were to learn.

Q. 'How was the world created?' A. 'By the word of God, for he commanded and it was made.'
Q. 'What space of time was the Almighty employed in the creation of the world?' A. 'Six days.'
Q. 'How long is it since the creation of the world?' A. 'Nearly six thousand years.'

Today, no such certainty is possible. Further, the methods of teaching encourage discussion and interpretation. Above all, the span of years separating teacher and pupils has contained a variety of dramatic changes. The children of the 1970s will grow up used to men on the moon, to life in orbit, to pocket-sized computers, but will be taught by some teachers who will have grown up in a world without television or radio. The rate of change makes each generation old-fashioned to the next and reduces the authority of the adult as a transmitter of culture, because that culture, in its technological aspects, is antiquated.[15]

Schools develop as societies grow complex and specialization within and between them is one part of a general differentiation of institutions. In large-scale, mobile, industrial societies schools increasingly become the means whereby individuals are prepared for, and allocated to, occupations. Simultaneously they are involved in the conflicts over values which accompany this complexity.

Part 2

A structural - functional model of the school

Introduction

A mother in her family, a student in his college, a worker in his factory, or anyone involved in an institution is in the wrong position to view it as a social organization. This requires a view of the whole, not obscured by personal involvement. It is the position adopted by the anthropologist in an alien culture. An approximation to this objectivity is essential for the scientific perspective. Ralph Linton once wrote that men are anthropoid apes trying to live like termites.[16] The social scientist tries to achieve a position similar to that of the entomologist examining an anthill. When he also uses the appropriate concepts and methods of investigation he is using a sociological perspective.

From such a position a school would seem to be a series of movements, activities and relationships, with a regular pattern, which would soon be predictable. Further, the participants would seem to have learnt a code whereby gestures, commands, positions, bells and other cues lead to new arrangements and relationships being taken up in different parts of the building and grounds. Groups form and reform around the school with few or no discernible instructions being given. Differences in response would be seen to distinguish two main groups, staff and pupils, with further divisions within each.

Observation of several schools would reveal an overall similarity of pattern. But consistent differences would be noticed in the pattern of activities and the relations between and within the groups. Closer observation would reveal differences between the schools in the expectations of staff and pupils. Each school would seem to have its own distinct climate or ethos and its own way of organizing its group life. These two aspects, culture and social structure, are convenient concepts for the analysis of any social organization.

Schools have been considered here as serving functions necessary for the whole society. But they can also be considered as social entities in their own right. This perspective refers, not so much to the individuals involved, as to the relations between them and the structures in the school through which these are determined. The focus will be on the way individuals are allocated to statuses and motivated to perform appropriate roles in them. Formal and informal arrangements are viewed as ensuring continuity, coordination and the achievement of goals, as well as involving and integrating staff and pupils. Each structure will be analysed through the function it serves in these processes which enable the school to persist as a social organization although staff and pupils come and go. Underlying this model is the assumption that individuals involved in the same culture come to share the same values and that the social structure dovetails individuals into an integrated system.

This structural-functional model, used in Chapters 2, 3 and 4, gives an idealized view of the school. This will be criticized and rectified in Part 3. Teachers and pupils do not work together without friction and many groups act to disrupt the working of the school rather than supporting it. However, the structural-functional model is valuable in showing why schools develop characteristic patterns of organization and why many features persist even though they appear to be irrelevant to contemporary circumstances. By temporarily ignoring the conflicts, factors underlying cooperation can be analysed. Few schools are so chaotic that the model has no relevance. Many approximate very closely to it.

2

The culture of the school

Speech-day references to a school as 'a happy place', 'a hive of industry', 'a Christian community', are comments on the culture. This is the total of material objects, values, knowledge and techniques which persists while waves of individuals pass through. To each of these individuals, the culture presents a set of meanings to be learnt. Once this is done they will feel 'at home', able to understand and respond in an appropriate way. It will be their school, good or bad but unique. They will be in a position to transmit these meanings to the next intake. The learning is mainly symbolic, words and cues and gestures rather than firsthand contact with objects or situations.

Schools, like other organizations are frequently described by their 'spirit', or 'ethos', or 'climate'. This is an attempt to sum up an impression, not of particular aspects, but of the total pattern of life, culture, within it. The building and equipment of schools may be identical, but their cultures differ, being the result of traditions built up by successive intakes of individuals, interacting with one another under the influence of patterns already established. Consequently old schools generally have a more pervasive culture. The persistence of these traditions in the older public schools exerts considerable influence over the pupils and sets limits for behaviour. 'It is a highly organized, almost a totalitarian community. For a society, its rules are strict, and personal freedom severely limited. It has a corporate religion and a corporate morality, together with a corporate tradition that may well be stronger than either.'[1]

The following scene was repeated daily in a secondary modern school. The boys would assemble in the school hall, chattering loudly, first and second years sitting on the floor, third and fourth forms on chairs behind them, and the fifth on chairs at the end of each row. As staff came in and sat on the stage the noise would diminish slightly. Occasionally a master would stand and walk to the front of the stage. The noise would stop, to rise again as he returned to his place. The arrival of the Senior Master left only a few boys at the back talking. Slowly he would remove his spectacles, place them in his top pocket and replace them with another pair. The action stilled the hall. The entry of the headteacher was the cue for all to stand. As he opened his prayer book, heads were bowed and the morning service began. The seating arrangements, movements, gestures were a language all knew, part of the regular, recurrent pattern of life, symbolic in the same way as the bowing of heads and the devotions that followed.

Culture as a design for living involves the individual with a series of such symbols. Once the correct responses to these have been learnt they can fit into the design. This is not only a matter of wearing a school uniform, singing the school song, performing elaborate rituals and ceremonies. An understanding of the cues and signals is necessary before correct responses are possible. An established junior school form with the same teacher for most of the day obeys many instructions which an outdated observer would neither see nor hear. The children know what is meant by the position taken up by the teacher, her facial expression, finger actions, tone of voice and other symbolic gestures. They also respond in similar ways to the actions of other pupils in the class, to the headteacher in the school hall and, in a small school, to all staff and most pupils in most situations. Each school, therefore, has a set of shared symbols which, when learnt, determine what to perceive and how to interpret it. Attention must be paid to certain gestures by staff but not others; this bell but not those noises. Children must learn that talking at the same time as one teacher will be always punished, but that it is safe with another except on Monday mornings. In this way a picture of the school is built up for those involved in it.

The design for living in a school takes the form of customs, traditions and unwritten laws which persist and affect successive intakes. Individuals fall into these ways and oppose those who violate them. In time vested interests in preserving them build up and reform is opposed. They may be protected by law, defended by the staff. More frequently they are enforced informally, through the sensitivity of individuals to the opinions and actions of others. The patterns of behaviour are, therefore, felt to be right. These standards or moral evaluations are norms. Pupils and staff come to see certain ways of behaviour as proper. Some become sacred and violations are viewed with horror. Others are held more lightly and punishments are without moral approbation. Behind the norms lie values which determine what is seen as right and wrong.

Thus the main aim of a school may be to increase knowledge or deepen intellectual understanding, but all schools go beyond this to try to spread ideas of right and wrong, a common morality. This direction or regulation of behaviour is normative, consisting of a series of social norms or constraints to act in clearly defined and sanctioned ways. The culture also influences the way people obtain pleasure or feel pain. Children arrive at school with ideas of beauty, good taste, fashion or music already partly determined, in ways that differ between different countries or regions and classes within them. At school these definitions are extended and modified. One school may lay emphasis on individual success, another on collective achievement. One may teach children to take pleasure in dancing, another in competitive sports. In some schools hymn-singing is enjoyed, in others hated. Thus all who are involved in a culture tend to be mindful of the same things, share the same pleasures, hold the same values and feel constrained by the same norms.

These influences on the way children perceive the world and evaluate it are strengthened by the image of the ideal school which is part of the British culture. Musgrave sees this as follows:[2]

1. A school should have independence and individuality.
2. A school should be small enough to have a common purpose and be under one head.
3. A school should mould character,
4. and therefore should transmit a definite set of values.

This is a model whose size, status and purpose combine to produce powerful cultural pressures on the pupils.

Once individuals have been exposed to a culture and have established friendships within it they will be motivated to act in clearly defined ways. It is this regulation and guiding of behaviour which accounts for the predictability visible to the observer. But culture is not a straitjacket, for the involvement of pupils and staff outside the school in systems having different values and norms, means that the school must work within limits imposed by the wider society. There will be degrees of involvement, so that some will be deeply identified with the school while others have only a superficial connection. Staff and pupils vary from the strict 9 a.m. to 4 p.m. clock-watcher to those who have to be told by the caretaker to leave. The former will remain insulated from cultural pressures, while the latter are often influenced by the school for the rest of their lives. The boarding school has a greater chance of making such an impact and the persistence of public school values into adult life results from this. Finally, individual differences in personality will result in degrees of conformity. The level of involvement is an index of the *esprit de corps*. In any social group, individual needs are satisfied by the action of others. The success of a school in satisfying these needs largely determines the level of involvement and consequently the motivation to learn the values and norms. Harmony and order can prevail as a consequence of need satisfaction rather than of imposed discipline.

Different cultures have evolved different styles of living. Culture defines the relation between the individual, as actor, to other actors and to the situation that they are in. Interaction or social action, where the behaviour of each person involved is influenced by the action of others, has been divided by T. Parsons into three types.[3] It is through being involved in these that individuals come to learn and share values and interact in orderly ways. The balance between them is a useful way of distinguishing between social groupings, for each will have its own distinctive pattern.

1. Instrumental action

This is directed at a future goal. The behaviour is a means to the end or ends, which may be very distant or the immediate result of the act. It is mainly cognitive and is the most obvious activity in schools. It includes the accumulation of knowledge, skills and attitudes which are necessary for passing examinations, getting good marks and a good job after leaving. But there is also activity instrumental in the wider socializing purposes of the school. It is orientated to turn out good pupils and good citizens. The goals often relate to behaviour as adults, and the children are organized in activities which will promote this.

2. Expressive action

This is a goal in itself. The actor expresses himself to satisfy his needs, which may be learned or innate. The action may release tensions or satisfy a desire to be creative, artistic, destructive. This can be seen in a school class expressing itself in dancing, painting or making music. Here there is no attempt to build up skills as the main purpose; each child is releasing energy from within himself, not absorbing information or practising techniques. Many activities in schools are spontaneous in this way, some being organized, some allowed to develop without action by staff. Both the theory and practice of primary education have increasingly stressed expressive action. Rousseau's *Emile*, which stimulated the movement towards child-centred education and the reform of traditional methods, was a plea for the priority of expressive over instrumental action for the young.[4]

3. Moral (normative) action

This is directed towards integrating groups through sharing common ideas of right and wrong. At the same time the individuals concerned are learning to be moral, capable of distinguishing between good and evil and acting on this. A school tries to be a consistent moral influence and much of its activity is designed to punish wrong and reward correct behaviour. The intention is to produce moral children, not just within school, but in their whole lives. This is why the school tries to exclude bad influences which detract from this effort.

The balance between these three forms of action is determined by the cultural values for which the school stands. While all lay emphasis on morality, the stress laid on instrumental and expressive activity varies widely. Generally the proportion of instrumental activity increases with the age of the children. The infant class may be entirely concerned with expressing itself, while the teacher intervenes only gradually to discipline the children for formal work to come. The sixth form of a grammar school rarely deviates from the examination syllabus. But each school establishes its own balance, ranging from the child-centred progressive school to the subject-centred and traditional. Further, although schools usually have an easily detectable balance, individual teachers may use very different methods within their own classrooms.

The examples that follow are based on notes taken while visiting schools and on questionnaires filled in by students working within them.[5] They have been selected from the many studied because they contrast with one another, not in being good, bad or representative, but in the goals they are trying to achieve and the way they are organized.

School A

This was a four-class infant school on the same site as a junior school, but only sharing playgrounds and kitchen. It was situated in an area of early Victorian terraced houses, in a large industrial town. The school was built in the 1930s and was externally un-attractive, yet it was very clean, newly painted and its interior was fresh, alive with pictures, flowers and children's paintings. The children were clean, polite and orderly.

The headmistress had impressed her personality and views on the whole school. She saw her task as one of promoting good habits which the children would not learn at home. Cleanliness, good manners, orderly behaviour and good taste were valued more than preparation for transition to the adjoining junior school. They were encouraged and rehearsed at assemblies, in plays, painting, flower arrangement, decoration and patient individual work with difficult children. The headmaster of the junior school complained of the lack of basic skills among children after transfer but his proposals were resisted. The school had a very high reputation in the community and more support from the parents than the area would have led one to expect.

School B

This was a one-form entry junior school in a small market town, taking children from a variety of backgrounds. It was housed in an old church hall on to which had been built a number of annexes, including a new prefabricated hut. The inside of the old part was dark and untidy with cupboards containing dusty books and models. The most striking feature of the school was its apparent lack of direction. Headteacher and staff were almost invisible, the school seeming to run without anyone in charge. Staff and children were relaxed and friendly and students found it exceptionally pleasant.

The children worked without being driven and settled down to individual reading or hobbies when they had finished any work set. Children not able to read or write got on with their own activities without guidance from a teacher. All movement was slow and haphazard but not noisy. Leaving the room to get the milk or to go to the toilet was done without asking the teacher. The brighter children got their share of grammar school places. In everything, children followed a routine which seemed as established as the heavy desks and vaulted ceilings.

School C

This was a three-stream entry, mixed secondary modern school in a large town. It was of modern glass and concrete construction. The children came mainly from a large council estate and semi-detached private estates. The children were all in uniform and were meticulous over their 'Sirs' and 'Ma'ams'. Movement in the corridors was precise, down the lefthand side, with prefects in the centre lane keeping order. The headmaster was forceful, busy about the school and with firm ideas about the value of good discipline and hard work.

The school had an impressive academic record even before the introduction of the C.S.E. Classes were carefully streamed and set, but the type of work was identical between streams. All followed a rigorous academic régime and a majority took some type of external examination. Few left before completing a fifth year and this indicated an appreciation of the school's efforts by parents. This had also resulted in their paying for extra library facilities. However traditional the régime, it was supported by staff, pupils and parents, and the hard-driving was not resented.

These examples show how the working and social life of schools can be governed by different ends and different means for their accomplishment. School B had no detectable aims, yet there were clearly established patterns of behaviour. Here the original goals had been lost, but the routine persisted. Schools A and C differed fundamentally in their values and organization. But this was not just due to the different ages of their pupils. They represent a fundamental division of aim and activity between schools at all levels. School A emphasized moral ends and expressive activity concentrating on promoting values useful in themselves. The staff were teaching a way of life and ensuring that individual children were not disturbed by this due to its difference from that experienced at home. Children were encouraged to express themselves through art, dance, play and in making the school attractive. Staff–pupil relations were close and children were judged for their personal qualities, rather than their academic performance. What they were, rather than what they did was important. Staff inevitably became closely involved with the children, accepting obligations as friends and social workers, as well as teachers.

School C emphasized instrumental activity, serving as a means to ensuring a good future for the children. Work was subject-centred, directed towards examinations which would give pupils access to good jobs. Staff assessed children through marks on tests and saw their job as instructors rather than welfare workers. Their obligations were confined to efficient teaching and scrupulous assessment. Behaviour problems were dealt with as barriers to good learning rather than symptoms of personality defects. The norms acted to produce hard work, obedience and competition.

Each of these schools had its own values and procedures. Some of these were deliberate policies, others had evolved over the years, without any central determination. All contained elements of all three modes of action, but each had its own priorities. Within them children were subject to norms which defined the roles they would play. Each school tried to get parental support for these definitions. Similarly teachers felt obliged to accept different curricula, different priorities and different responsibilities. Within limits set by the normative pressures, staff and pupils will interpret their role in their own way, but each is still contained within a system geared to particular role performances, which limits their freedom.

The culture of a school persists as an influence on anyone joining it, while continually being reshaped by the participants. To the newcomer it is a pattern to which he has to adjust. Only when it has been learnt can he feel at home. This is the cause of unease, discomfort felt by the new pupils or staff; it is the time when mistakes are made. It is especially hard on those joining after the year's work has started, for they have missed the routine which helps in learning the culture. The tears, breakdowns and reluctance to leave mother as the infant first arrives in the reception class are partly the ignorance of what goes on in a school. But a similar and often equally dramatic, if less obvious, tension is experienced whenever there is transition to a new class, or to a new school.[6]

Once the culture has been learnt, the situation loses its strangeness. The actions of others become meaningful and predictable; everything falls into place as the newcomer slips into the routine. In sociological terms, the situation has been structured for him and he has learnt his role. He is no longer an outsider, no longer hesitant and uncertain. Soon the values and norms are known. There is a common sharing of symbols, a common basis for the perception of events, shared sources of pleasure and pain, and similar ideas of right and wrong.

The culture of a school, however, rarely consists of common values shared by staff and pupils. Not only does each class and group within the classes develop its own values, but there is a division between the official values and those held informally. Staff and pupils have their own standards which they use 'backstage', out of sight, as well as the official ones for use 'onstage' when others can see them.[7] Teachers who inadvertently overhear pupils talking soon realize the gap between ideal and reality, 'foreground' and 'underground'. But they too relax into informal attitudes once in the privacy of the staffroom. Both these parts of the culture have to be learnt.

School cultures also reflect the society in which they operate, or those agencies responsible for them. The religious motive has dominated the history of English education. Before the State intervened in 1870, the three most productive agencies providing education were the Society for the Propagation of Christian Knowledge, The British and Foreign School Society and The National Society for Promoting the Education of the Poor in the Principles of the Established Church Throughout England and Wales. All religions have used education to teach the young those values and habits which they uphold, but education is also an instrument in political indoctrination. Not only is this prevalent in totalitarian states, but it is the way feelings of nationhood are built up in newly independent countries or those, such as the U.S.A., where large numbers of immigrants had to be absorbed.

More generally, schools are part of the wider culture and share its values. The schools of the eighteenth century reflected the paternalistic, static, preindustrial era. They taught children of the poor to know their place and to behave themselves in it. The rich man was in his castle, the poor were to be contented at his gate. Today children are prepared for a series of examinations that will sort them into different statuses. They are exposed to the pressures of a more mobile society while young. Infant School A had deliberately excluded these influences, but in Junior School B the children brought them into school themselves, some working hard to pass the selection examination, without apparent pressure from the staff. School C was organized to exploit competition.

Schools, as agencies for transmitting culture, are inevitably involved in creating commitment to the values of adult working and social life as these are seen by teachers. In the words of the Plowden Committee, 'Schools exist to foster virtuous circles'.[8] These may not be shared by all sections of the community. Where a child is exposed to contradictory values in school and home, the resulting culture conflicts often lead to his dissociating himself from the school. More rarely it may ultimately lead to rejecting the way of life of his parents. This is particularly relevant when a working class child from a family which is itself relatively uneducated, enters a grammar school. The high wastage among such children has been indicative of the conflict they have met.[9]

The life of children outside the school can therefore reinforce them in opposition to its values. Informal groups establishing their own subcultures within a school can give meanings to the symbols of the school far removed from those intended by the staff. The school song is parodied, prayers and hymns debased, friendly gestures by staff seen as weakness and changes in traditional teaching methods taken as a cue for creating chaos. A school stresses selected values. It excludes the ugly and evil and concentrates on the beautiful and good. But children can resist this influence if supported by groups inside and influences elsewhere. Morals, manners and taste can be derided as well as copied. Unfortunately, this is often difficult to detect as the resistance is concealed beneath a veneer of conformity.

Even the most timid infant in the reception class brings to school an accumulation of learning that enables him to perceive and interpret the school in a unique way. None is a passive recipient of group pressures which mould him. All will learn to play their roles in a way that will make predictable, reciprocal action possible through the pressure of the norms. But degrees of freedom remain even in the harshest penal institution. In most, only those parts which are vital to the running of the institution leave little margin for individual freedom. Elsewhere, latitude increases as the activity becomes less essential. In schools, silence is enforced when teacher is speaking in class, but not in the playground. Some examinations are set and marked externally to avoid recognition of particular pupils, but homework marking may be adjusted to take into account a handicap suffered by someone. Frequently a group may combine to 'work the system'. In no case is culture a strait jacket.

This individual freedom within the culture can also be used by teachers to establish their own aura of friendliness, strictness or weakness. Pupils learn to behave in ways defined by the teacher once they enter his lesson. Here they can relax, there 'it's all go'. A joke here is sacrilege, there it's one long laugh. Staff as well as pupils can establish subcultures. In one boys' secondary school, the senior master's room was pervaded by such an air of order, whether he was present or not, that new teachers taking difficult classes were often given it, in the knowledge that within it, the most rebellious boy was restrained. The conditions under which order and predictability will result are still the same, all must learn and share the same meanings of events, objects and symbols. Individuals switch from one set of meanings to another as they pass from one subculture to another.

Schools, like other institutions, differ in the degree of consensus over the values within them. A prison has few areas of agreement between staff and prisoners, but in a church, priest and worshippers may exhibit perfect consensus. Similarly, some schools are seen by pupils as something to be endured for as short a time as possible. others gain the affections of their pupils. Frequently these feelings persist into adult life. Some look back with hatred, while others wear the old school tie and retain a sentimental attachment. This is again open to individual interpretation, for the same school can inspire feelings of dislike and affection. In one secondary school, while a new cricket pavilion was awaiting its ceremonial opening after being paid for by grateful old scholars, others dug up the cricket square in the night.

Boarding schools, with their greater exposure to the culture, frequently inspire great loyalty, but can equally produce intense dislike. Small rural primary schools such as School B in the examples quoted earlier, often have a sense of identity missing in the impersonal, larger urban school. This is probably reinforced by the personality of young children. As children grow older, the attractions outside the school weaken its power to hold interest and affection.

Much of the everyday work of the school is concerned with building up identification with it and with the values for which it stands. There must be exposure to influences which will make pupils feel a pride in belonging to the school and a commitment to the principles which it serves. There is no division between these, for any activity involving pupils in the latter will also reinforce the former. The morning act of worship is designed to promote Christian belief. But the ritual involved is a communal act, an expression of shared values, and will serve to consolidate any sense of unity. Those who reject the school will usually have rejected the religious, moral and social values which support it. Those who identify with the school are more likely to have also accepted supporting values.

This illustration shows the way consensus and commitment are inculcated. First, there are communal acts, second, these involve ritual behaviour and third, they are rich in symbolism. All these expose the individual to cultural pressures. This is not always the manifest purpose of the activity. The morning assembly is designed for worship and to communicate the day's arrangements to the whole school, but beneath these are hidden, latent functions promoting social solidarity, increasing the feeling of belonging.[10]

Schools abound in communal activities. The formal organization into classes guarantees that all are continually involved in acting as a group. For most of the school day they will be treated as a class, as juniors or seniors or prefects, as a year group, or as the school. They are praised and punished in a group, answer as a class, play as a team. School outings, sports days, organized holidays, parades or assemblies to mark special events, matches against old students or parents, consolidate the school through shared activity, particularly where this is in the public eye. Even school meals in appropriate conditions can serve this function. In boarding schools the opportunities are multiplied.

Frequently these activities are in contrast to or competition with other schools. School teams consolidate in the face of opponents and supporters get emotionally involved. The results are read out to the school with congratulations or hopes for improvements. Children who were friends in the same primary school, after arbitrary allocation to different schools, come to see each other as strange and often hostile. Once integrated into different school cultures, with different values, they lose the basis of past friendship.

Some school activity is deliberately designed to promote solidarity. Headteachers are pleased to announce in assembly that a local notable has remarked on how well members of the school conduct themselves in public. An offender is not only guilty personally, but has let the school down. The culmination of these efforts is on Open or Speech Day, when the school is on show and all the year's successes are recalled in public and the school is committed to improve on this next year.

This communal activity is invariably ritualistic. Ritual reinforces common beliefs and commitment to the norms. This accounts for its presence in all institutions, particularly religious, where these are vital. Ritual as part of the culture is divisible into formal and informal elements, for 'backstage' ritual is as common as that organized by the staff. In many older schools, the origins of these informal rituals lie buried, but they still exert a powerful influence. Prefects may walk with a cane, white waistcoats may be worn if a boy has his colours, seniors may leave waistcoat buttons undone, the stone lions by the school gates must be saluted, juniors must raise their caps when passing prefects. In all schools similar rituals, slang and rites tend to emerge.[11]

Most of the formal activities of the school are also ritualized. Classes rise when a teacher first enters the room and wait to be told to sit. In many schools the class chants 'Good morning Miss X' and waits for the response. She replies with the dignity appropriate to her position and gives the signal for them to sit down. The register is produced and solemnly marked with the customary strokes and circles. Notes are produced by those returning after absence. The class files out of the room to take up set positions in the hall ready for the morning ceremonies. In large schools this is often in a definite sequence of classes to avoid disorder. Throughout the day movement and interaction are prescribed, formalized into customary patterns. Staff and children are caught up in a series of actions which are repeated day after day.

Even more important is the existence of cultural symbols. Schools tend to develop their own emblems, signs, words and actions that represent the school or aspects of it. These are shared by those who are involved in the culture, learnt by newcomers and preserved in the minds of some of those who have left. To all, the school tie summons up pictures of the school in the minds of those who see it, some pleasant, some unpleasant. The school song, for all its naïvety can bring a lump to the throat of some; others recall it in anger. Symbols act as a focus for emotions as well as standing for objects or ideas.

It is the sharing of symbols that brings a feeling of being at home in a particular culture and which consequently promotes unity. Culture can be seen as shared symbols and their definitions.[12] In a school, acts, gestures, words, bells, chants, special hymns and prayers, indeed a whole range of communications, stand for something that is recognized and meaningful to staff and pupils. A well-run primary school class, having the same teacher for a year, develops a set of shared symbols which enable it to work without many instructions. When a student teacher takes over the class, her ignorance of the culture and its symbols means that instructions must now be given. Children used to responding to a wave of a hand or a nod of the head, now get confused by their absence. Only when a new common 'language' is learnt does a smooth routine return. Dilke lists 126 'notions', words or phrases forming such a language at Winchester.[13] Each newcomer is taught the lore and vocabulary through being assigned to another who has already been there a year.

A secondary school assembly hall is often crowded with overt symbols of the school and its culture. The headteacher's chair is large, centrally placed in front of a row of ordinary ones for the staff. He wears a gown and all stand when he appears. Pictures of founders, the Queen and past headteachers hang on the walls. Above the stage is the school badge and motto. In a cupboard on a side wall are the cups and shields won by the school or by its houses. Seating arrangements symbolize the status of staff and various forms of pupils. Here, surrounded by emblems of the school, pupils are constantly reminded of its importance and their part in it. This is accompanied not only by the visible authority of the staff but by the religious observances which occur there. The solemnity of the proceedings and surroundings serves to create an atmosphere similar to that in a church, emotionally preparing the individual for a re-affirmation of faith.

In larger schools, where identification is difficult due to the numbers involved, houses often serve as intermediate focuses. In very large comprehensive schools, where many important activities take place in the house, it attains cultural autonomy and pupils can feel a primary loyalty to it, rather than to the school itself. House colours, badges, sports shirts symbolize it in its competition with the others. A class within a school can also develop into a sub-culture. This is easier where there is a lack of movement between it and the other forms, or class teaching as in the primary school. The lowest stream, with its special teacher in secondary schools, with the need to create a sense of security, can also become a particular centre of affection. The result is often to give school leavers the idea that theirs was a unique class, sometimes to the extent of forming a society or group to preserve their links.

These generalizations about culture have neglected four important factors. First, individuals, due to differences in personality and background are involved in the culture of a school in a variety of ways. Second, school cultures conflict in various ways with their environments, and staff and pupils are involved in both, subject to conflicting demands. Third, within each school there are many contrasting value and normative systems. Staff and pupils, onstage and backstage, different formal and informal groupings, develop their own blueprints. Any one individual will be involved in more than one, and in the conflicts due to exposure to contrasting values.

Fourthly, a heavy turnover of staff reduces the chance of a pervasive, powerful culture emerging. Staff have to absorb the culture before they can support and extend it. Where there is little continuity, staff do not have time to become committed to the school and do not reinforce its efforts. Difficult schools are often used for temporary posts while waiting for a more promising opportunity to turn up. They also have a high proportion of supply teachers and part-time staff and both can weaken the impact of the school. Unfortunately these internal weaknesses result from poor environments and reduce the chances of the school having any beneficial effect. These schools also have absences above average, particularly among those children whose backgrounds are worst. This further reduces their influence.

The net result of being involved in the culture is to make things meaningful. The action, the cues and the beliefs are difficult for the outsider to understand. They are understood and natural to those involved. Where people know what to expect in a situation it is structured for them. To say that a school is an institution is to say that participants will not only be behaving in predictable ways, but that they will think of these ways as right. Culture is learnt and shared, and enables individuals to act together without disruptive conflicts. The effect of being continually treated as a member of a unique school community is to make the pupil a part of it. We tend to see ourselves as others treat us.

This learning, therefore, produces the sentiments of belonging that bind the school together and make it a persistent influence in the life of those involved. This has important practical implications. Many of the ceremonial, ritual practices appear superficial and naïve. But they may be necessary if the school is to become a community and have an influence on its pupils. They may be the channel through which the values for which the school stands are transmitted. Just as the flag, playing the national anthem at public meetings and the recall of past national triumphs help individuals to identify with the nation, so similar symbols and ceremonies help to build up school spirit. To prune these because adult reason sees them as anachronistic in the twentieth century may be to destroy an important source of motivation, involvement and identification.

3

The social structure of the school

A culture is a way of life, which when learnt, defines the situation for all who share it, so they can communicate and respond to one another. But individuals do not just learn common values and norms; they learn those which apply to the positions they occupy. Within a school, staff, children, caretaker, cooks and cleaners, must play their part in the right way, at the right time and place, if useful work is to be done. There must be arrangements for allocating them to their positions or statuses, teaching them the behaviour that will be expected of them, making sure they are rewarded for correct, and punished for wrong, behaviour and for regulating the relations between them. These arrangements are the social structure or organization.

The orderly patterns of social life and the predictable responses of one person to another indicate that individuals have learnt to play parts. These are roles, each learnt by individuals in their positions in the division of labour. Thus a child aged five years has already learnt the role of son or daughter in a family, but soon has to learn the new role of pupil within the organization of a particular school. In a school, headteacher, staff and pupils of various ages occupy clearly defined statuses and interact in clearly defined ways. These definitions or expectations have been shown to derive from the culture of the school, for the roles consist of social norms regulating the behaviour of anyone in a particular status or position.

Joining an organization or changing status within it, means learning a new role. This means learning the norms which define the behaviour expected of persons in this position. Once the culture has been internalized, the norms will act to reduce indiscretions and mistakes to a minimum. The individual will not only know the correct behaviour but will perform the role without any need for frequent, conscious reference to the rules governing it. A child has to learn a variety of roles within education as infant, junior, secondary pupil, leader, subordinate, monitor, prefect, apprentice and student.

Sociologists, unlike psychologists, are concerned with these statuses and roles, rather than with the individuals who perform them. They are interested in the common behaviour patterns of teachers, fathers and so on rather than the particular behaviour of any one of them. They examine the values and norms which shape the roles and the way people are allocated to the statuses. They look at the way the roles are learnt, and the forces which inhibit deviations from them. They analyse the way that tensions and conflicts arise, and how they are resolved. They investigate the way the roles change, due to influences from within or outside the structure. In a school, therefore, the sociologist looks at regular predictable patterns of behaviour by staff and pupils, and the relations between them. To do this he employs his own concepts, particularly that of role, and remains as detached an observer as possible.

While individuals feel constrained to abide by the definition of the role which applies to their position, they also amend it by their personal interpretation. A teacher is expected to behave in particular ways, but may add personal touches. A bow tie, high heels, corduroy jacket, short skirt, close relations with pupils, mild swearing and other eccentricities can serve, within limits, to carve out a personal social status. A teacher is expected to behave within well-defined limits, but on a school staff interpretations vary. On the same staff are the square and the swinging, the autocrat and the egalitarian, the traditionalist and the progressive. Positional status, and the role expected of persons in such positions, form a framework in which personal status, and personal versions of the role, can be established. Similarly there may be a pupil's role, but each will establish his own version within the limits set by the social structure of the school. Some schools lay down rigid codes of behaviour, others allow considerable latitude.

Because many schools, like most modern organizations, are large, individuals rarely know all of the working arrangements. They occupy a status and perform the appropriate role with possibly little idea of what goes on in the headmaster's office or in the playground. The children accept a routine without a part in its determination. The caretaker may not realize the inconvenience to staff when he insists on the classrooms being cleaned as soon as school finishes. The headmaster may issue instructions with little idea of the differences between the classes through which they operate.

Norms not only define the role to be performed by persons in each status, but restrain anyone from adopting a role which is inappropriate. A pupil who walked into the staffroom, lit a cigarette and made ribald remarks about the head would be rapidly ejected and punished. Groups operate smoothly only if allocation to a status, learning of the appropriate role and regulation of the relations between persons of different statuses are efficient.

Sex and age are the most common basis for a division of labour. Some societies ascribe status according to personal qualities such as father's status, skin colour, religion or physical appearance, while others lay more emphasis on achievements such as examination results, technical skill or athletic ability. Allocation within schools contains elements of achievement and ascription. What you do is important as well as who you are. Performance and personal qualities are taken into account. Staff are appointed on the basis of qualification, experience and skill, but personal qualities are important, both on interview for the post and later while teaching. Similarly pupils are allocated to a school because they live near by, are the right age and have the appropriate ability. But they also rely on personal qualities to improve their chances of selection and promotion.

However, both staff and pupils in their positions in the school find that their behaviour in relation to each other is laid down in advance by their own expectations and by demands on them by others. These rights and obligations define the role they will play. They will not only feel constrained to behave in a certain way, but will come to feel that this is the correct behaviour. The norms which define the roles are moral demands which, when learnt, make deviations unlikely because of the feeling of being wrong which will result. Playing the role of assistant teacher, or head, or monitor or junior, frequently leads to it being enjoyed, seen as natural and right. The prefect may be embarrassed when first promoted, but soon grows into the part, enjoys his privileges and takes his duties seriously. The first months of teaching can be a trial, but this usually changes into a feeling of being at home. Like an actor, individuals fit into their role. A new headmaster may feel that a thrashing he is about to give will 'hurt me more than it hurts you', but his distaste is subjugated to what he feels to be right. Soon he becomes less upset as caning is built into his repertoire. Similarly, once he is treated as powerful, surrounded by all the trappings of his office, he will take on the characteristics of authority, even if he has not anticipated this before appointment. Similarly staff adjust to the normative pressures of the role. Even the most unpromising student teacher may blossom once in full command in the classroom and confound the opinions of his ex-tutors.

The roles played in any institution are coordinated. This results from the common origins of the norms which define the roles and constrain people in them. In a utopia all will share the same values, all will be regulated by the same norms, and roles will be perfectly synchronized. At the other extreme is the state of complete anomy, normlessness, disorder, wherein there is no consensus over values. Real life situations usually lying between, are those in which there is enough consensus and regulation to ensure sufficiently smooth working, but in which there is also continual stress. Schools are in this mean position of a culture, homogeneous enough to ensure relatively smooth working, but heterogeneous enough to create continual conflicts, even if mostly trivial. In addition, schools are affected by outside influences, which can be both sympathetic and critical. The roles of head, teachers, and pupils, will therefore, have a common basis, but will rarely dovetail perfectly. There will always be areas where the roles grind in friction like faulty gears.

This can be illustrated by using the division between instrumental and expressive action discussed earlier. A grammar school concentrating on its 'A' level results will be organized to increase instrumental performance. Teachers and pupils will interact in a formal, neutral way, within a narrow field of activity, concentrating

on each other's performance. Textbooks, straight factual transmission and objective, competitive examinations, play a major
part in this education. Staff and pupils will be specialists, concentrating their energies on a narrow front. Broader objectives are
subordinated to the job of ensuring examination success. Motivation
is maintained through stress on work as a means to examination
success. But many will object to this and press for a more liberal
approach.

A progressive junior school is liable to place most value on satisfying the emotional needs of children. Education of the 'whole child'
is the goal. Relations are consequently affective and based on
personal qualities. Games, art, movement, self-expression, participation in joint activities play a large part in the school day. Staff and
pupils will accept diffuse obligations, involving themselves in a
whole range of activities. Motivation will come from the satisfaction
of needs through this activity and through personal attention. But
parents and staff may be anxious for more direct help in passing the
secondary selection examination and for a less diffuse approach to
the acquisition of knowledge.

Motivation is largely determined by the factors outside the control of the school. Families push with different strengths, and opportunities for employment exert different pressures. But the social
structure of the school is also important. Children are continually
being allocated by teachers through marking, reporting, streaming,
promoting, relegating and selecting. Each placement affects the
child's perspective of himself in the education system. Allocation
to the 'D' stream produces the 'D' stream mentality, just as
masculine behaviour comes through being treated as a boy. Being
in an 'A' stream class raises levels of aspiration. The social structure
is not only an organization of positions and a regulating of the relation between them, it is a determinant of horizons and prospects.
Playing a role soon leads to an adjustment of the person to it.[1]

Lacey,[2] in a study of a boys' grammar school, has shown how a
class organized itself into statuses, after an initial period of random
interaction. In the unstreamed first year, popularity went with
academic achievement. But after streaming in the second year,
academic success and striving was no longer a basis for popularity

in the third, 'C' stream. The new leaders in this form were those holding subcultural, antischool values. In Lacey's terms, differentiation (streaming) by the staff, had polarized the boys into those holding pro-school and anti-school values. The leaders in both extreme groups were selected for completely opposite qualities by their peers. Division by streaming had produced two systems of status. Hargreaves[3] found the same results of streaming in his study of a secondary modern school. These results were not perceived by the staff of the school.

This tendency for people to settle into the status which they have been allocated, lies at the base of all objections to streaming and selection. The decision of the teachers who select or stream is always proved right, because after the decision the children take on the attitudes and consequently the performance of their new group. The action produces just those results which were predicted.[4]

This illustrates the usefulness of distinguishing between the intended and the unintended consequences of actions. The manifest, intended function of allocating to different schools or streams within schools, may be to increase teaching efficiency. But its unintended, latent consequences can be to divide pupils up into pro- and anti-school factions and determine their attitudes to authority generally. The implication of this is that teachers are not only organizing school work, but are influencing the children's whole perception of education and their outlook in adult life.

The sociometric test, based on children's preferences for each other's company in various activities, can illustrate aspects of the social structure of a school class. The pattern of choices, concentrated on stars, avoiding isolates, linking small cliques, illustrates the arrangement of statuses at any one time in social activity. Not only are children being allocated by staff for academic purposes, they are arranging themselves informally. In Lacey's study these reinforced each other in the top stream, but clashed in the lower. But in both cases the individual child was placed by others in a position in which he would be treated as leader, lieutenant, isolate, clown, swot, scholar, dunce and so on. Defined and treated by others as a type, forced to play a role not written by him, the individual is subject to pressures which affect his identity as well as his performance.

This has been illustrated by a study of five-year-olds in a kindergarten group.[5] In playing together, the children adopted positions of dominance or submission. Four children achieved dominant positions, but in different ways. One was a technical virtuoso, teaching others how to play. Another was a diplomat involving other children in mutually satisfying games. Another dominated by force. Another tried to get his own way by breaking up the games. Yet another isolated himself from the group altogether. The rest of the children, while having their own pecking order, submitted to the suggestions of the more dominant group. At this early age, not only had differences emerged, but the social situation of play had been set in a way that gave the leaders, the isolates, the gangsters and the followers the appropriate statuses. Slowly these will be accepted, seen to be natural and the individuals will learn roles that may persist through school and into adult life.

Blyth,[6] reports

. . . at the age of 7, the detailed pattern of social relationships will tend to be rather shapeless and unstable, as they are among infants, though there is sometimes evidence of the beginnings of something more structured. The two sexes are also noticeably beginning to concentrate their choices within their own ranks. One year later, when they are between 8 and 9, this tendency has already become marked and thereafter it continues to intensify. . . . Thus the most usual situation is that at the end of the junior school years a marked focal group of boys, and a less marked group of girls, holds the centre of the social stage, while minorities, especially of girls, occupy the periphery.

Within these groups children have clearly defined statuses.

The most detailed study of older children has been Gordon's study of Wabash High School.[7] Not only did he find that there was a differentiation among the pupils which gave each a number of statuses according to their clique memberships, but this was an important source of motivation. The behaviour of these adolescents was largely determined by their need to sustain their standing in these informal groups. Coleman in another American study has confirmed this tendency for academic achievement to carry little weight as a motivator.[8] While teachers behave in a classroom as if their actions were the key factor in determining the children's response, the real motive may be in the relations within the class. Once a pupil has grown into his role, he interprets the teacher's actions from this viewpoint. However, American studies may have little relevance to the British situation.

The roles

The headmaster in Britain exercises personal power beyond that found in other countries. School policy and organization are largely within his control and his authority is complete. His obligations are: first, to be impartial, not giving favours to particular staff or pupils; second, to defend his staff against any outside interference in their work; third, to identify completely with his school. This is symbolized by his position above the battle, in his own study, in the large chair at the front of the stage, taking prayers and determining serious punishments. He is served by a secretary and is at the centre of all communications from outside. This gives him great potential power, but he is still dependent on others carrying out his orders, and consequently must not sacrifice their inherent goodwill.

In the small primary school, the teaching head has less opportunity to establish such a position. He is more involved with staff and pupils as persons, is called by his Christian name or 'Mr Smith' rather than 'Sir'. But he must still support his staff against criticism from outside, still be impartial, still be committed to the school. His role now overlaps with that of his staff, and lacks the symbolic trappings and the isolation of the non-teaching head in a large school. On the other hand, he is in a position to impress his personality on the whole school at first hand. He can take on pastoral responsibilities for his children, knowing the background and characteristics of each. But close relations with staff or pupils depend on their not taking advantage of the close relationship, and he must still be objective when assessing them for outside purposes. Again, the obligations and rights of the role are reciprocal.

The headteacher's status is usually separated from others in the school by a wide social distance. In a large school he can be a distant, patriarchal, Arnoldian figure, always at the centre of ceremonies. The pupil waits outside his door until a green light flashes or a distant voice is heard to say 'Come in'. Inside he has a large desk, with a small seat in front on which visitors sit. His decisions are made after reference to papers to which he alone has access. Again, the primary head establishes less distance, because he lacks these facilities and because the education of the young is less formally organized and gives less opportunity for status symbolism. In all cases the head is subject to strong normative pressures. He symbolizes the school to outsiders, and authority to the pupils. His freedom within these positions is limited, even though he has such a large degree of autonomy. Indeed, because he is in the central position of the school culture he is most involved in its values and norms. Above all he must support his staff. Becker[9] in a study of teachers in Chicago expressed this limitation as follows: 'But this acceptance of superiority has limits. Teachers have a well-developed conception of just how and towards what ends the principal's authority should be used, and conflict arises when it is used without regard for the teachers' expectations.'

Teachers too are constrained by norms. They are expected to dress respectably, behave impeccably and check bad behaviour among children. The role has changed not only because of changing educational theory and practices, but because the social conditions which have been primarily responsible for this have altered the teachers' authority and influence. Progressive, child-centred methods, in which the learner is active, rule out excessive authoritarianism. Every step away from the purely one way, chalk and talk methods derived from the monitorial system, closes the gap between class and teacher. While the primary school child retains his interest in the school, this does not create tensions, but at the secondary stage, it is just those schools, or classes within schools, that have the children most motivated to work, that have the most formal, examination-dominated teaching. The teaching role is less clearly defined in those secondary schools where lower stream children sometimes see little purpose in coming to school, but official recommendations call for flexible, outward-looking teaching. There is a discrepancy between the ideal and what the teachers feel is practicable.

B. Wilson has analysed the teaching role as diffuse and many-sided, among professions that increasingly call for only specific, narrowly defined obligations; concerned with values amid the growing prestige given to instrumental activity; emotionally involved, compared with the usually neutral professional relationship.[10] The relation between doctor and patient, or lawyer and client is essentially neutral, based on laws and codes and limited to the specific issue in hand. The lawyer who gets emotionally involved with his clients, adapts the laws to suit each case and tries to sort out their domestic problems at the same time will be disbarred. But the teacher has to combine these elements.

This inevitably creates role conflicts. Frequently, concern with children's personal problems is necessary to remove barriers to effective learning. Yet the teacher is continually selecting between children, grading them, determining their future life chances. He has to be simultaneously involved and detached. Such incompatible demands are a source of tension. The more sides there are to the role, the more chance it has of containing such conflicts. In addition, teachers are one group of many concerned with education. The teacher is involved with his colleagues, his head, parents, aides, governors, managers, inspectors, local authority and social workers, as he does his job. In his status as teacher he is involved with these, his role set. They will be sometimes reinforcing his efforts, but inevitably making contradictory demands. Role conflict, therefore, occurs partly through different definitions of the role which the individual may find irreconcilable. But conflicting demands can also come from the different persons in the role set. In both cases the conflicts are built into the role, structurally determined, not a fault of the individual occupying the status.

Relations between staff are also clearly defined. In secondary schools, senior assistants, heads of houses or departments, have an officially recognized position, but in primary schools, with class teaching, there is no such distinction. Age, experience, length of time in the school, and outstanding personal qualities can also be a basis for prestige. In addition, staff may divide into groups of men or women, married or single, as well as by age or seniority. These divisions are often recognized by seating arrangements or informal groupings in the staffroom, or in procedures such as morning assembly, lunch or tea-drinking. Relations and positions are predetermined, as a newcomer who sits in the wrong chair, uses the wrong locker or drinks from the wrong cup soon realizes. But however divided the staff are internally, they present a common front to outside criticism, particularly where this concerns their authority with children.

The relation between teachers and their pupils is determined by the norms which prescribe the role. First, although it is often necessary to establish close, affective relations with pupils, the norm is that there should be no familiarity. However friendly the teacher, there is never complete equality, and usually the norms of a school define an attitude of deference by the pupils. The distance between staff and pupils is maintained by making most situations in which the two meet formal enough to stop anyone stepping across the line. The class may murmur approval at a new hair style, dress or sports car, but the teacher acknowledges this gracefully and diverts the discussion into safer channels. This gap is usually defined as wide, narrowing after school in clubs, on the sports field, but separating again in the classroom, during academic work. Teachers who are too close to pupils are suspect by staff and pupils, while pupils who are familiar are punished.

Social distance also serves to maintain the control of staff over pupils. Teachers are expected to be in command at all times. Failure to retain this control is condemned by fellow staff, is a symptom of bad teaching to the pupils, and is the first index of failure to inspectors and others outside the school. It is the most worrying aspect of teaching to the student in training. The teaching role is defined first in terms of maintaining authority. This is part of the common front built up by a staff, which is threatened if any members fraternize too much or lose control.

This social distance is part of the general formality of the school. The school years, term, week and day are arranged so that at any one time many activities of staff and pupils are predetermined. The rights and obligations of children are defined according to the form they are in. Movement up the school is based on age. Children are grouped arbitrarily for the convenience of the teacher. The rooms in the school have clearly defined purposes, often supported by actual school rules. Children are categorized by form, house, measured ability or are ranked in performance. The formal relations between staff and pupils are one aspect of this. When a boy raises his cap or calls a master 'Sir', he is following the lines of behaviour laid down for him. But so is the headmaster as he punishes a child, or a mistress as she corrects one who is running in the corridor. Formality is the basis of the order that is necessary for education to go on.

Gabriel,[11] in an inquiry into teachers' attitudes, found that 'only a very small percentage of teachers' would welcome reforms such as less academic and freer timetables, more group work, abolition of examinations, loosening-up of discipline, and the involvement of the children in the organization of the school. Further, few schools were organized in any but a formal way, yet 63 per cent of this sample were in infant or primary schools. Taylor, in his study of the Secondary Modern School[12] also stressed the authoritarian nature of most teaching, particularly among newer teachers. The overwhelming support for retaining corporal punishment is another symptom.

The pupil's role is determined by normative pressures slowly built up through the school career of the child, so that the family atmosphere of the infants changes into the rigidity of the secondary school. This occurs in a series of stages arranged by age. Every year the child and his peers go up to another class and receive new privileges and responsibilities. Each raising of the school-leaving age, each new form which stays on voluntarily beyond the school-leaving age, increases the demand for the relaxation of school rules designed for children. But the relation between staff and pupils, formalized to guarantee a gap between them, cannot be changed easily. Once all fifth formers have rights to dress at will and are free from normal timetable commitments, the basis of staff authority is threatened unless they can be seen as distinct from the rest of the school. This is why a separate wing is desirable. A sixth form is a

minority, carrying responsibilities and doing work which differenti-
ates it from the rest of the school. If a whole year group is to be
given separate treatment, it must be seen to be outside the rules
which apply to the rest, if the present basis of school life is to persist.

The progressive definition of the role is in terms of obedience,
punctuality, attentiveness, industry and drive. Each school will have
its own balance between characteristics. All, however, stress loyalty
to the school, hard work and healthy activity. School mottoes give
an indication of these norms. 'Cheerfulness with industry', 'A sound
mind in a healthy body', 'Manners maketh man', 'Virtue, learning,
manners', indicate the direction in which the values operate. The
situation within the school is structured to ensure that pupils are
continually subjected to pressures underlying these definitions.

The pupils, like the staff, divide into informal groups. These become more permanent with age and the basis of friendship may
change. Blyth had shown how relations in school among primary
children are influenced by their distribution in the neighbourhoods
from which they come.[13] Further, these groups tended to bring
neighbourhood values into the school with them. Fathers' occupation did not seem to be an important factor in deciding the friends
in school of these young children. But children from very poor
and very rich areas, through associating with those in their own
neighbourhood and through parental influence, inevitably separate
into exclusive groups. By the secondary stage, socio-economic differences are recognized by the pupils and increasingly form the
basis of associations. Indeed, because socio-economic status affects
motivation and performance in school, selection and streaming tend
to divide children into groups of similar backgrounds.

Very often this informal social structure, with its own subculture,
operating backstage, provides a different definition and different
normative pressures. Webb has analysed one school in terms of a
guerrilla war between official pressure for docility and the informal
pressures to self-expression.[14] Hargreaves has shown how boys in
the lower streams of a secondary modern school rejected the values
of the school.[15] Consequently pupils too are subject to conflicting
definitions of their role. Frequently this involves a choice between

rejecting school values or rejecting their standing with their friends.

This is why prefects and monitors cannot carry their delegated authority very far. They are not insulated as are the staff, and cannot maintain any great social distance. A prefects' room may help, but they must also mix as equals and are continually challenged by backstage leaders who have the backing of some pupils against the school. However, Blyth has shown how prefects in a junior school could be chosen on their position in the children's informal groups using sociometric tests.[16] Follow-up of their performance showed that this was a valid method of choice. Some secondary schools also allow pupils to vote for their own leaders, particularly for minor posts and games.

This split in the school structure enables a similar solidarity to appear among pupils as among staff. The cultural definition of the teachers' role restrains them from establishing too intimate relations with pupils. Children seek a similar area of privacy and detachment. This builds up from the family atmosphere of the nursery class, until in the secondary school, the child who allows a teacher to become too friendly is subject to ridicule. The values of the backstage culture come to insist on group solidarity against 'them' just as 'they' present a united front from the staffroom. The junior school child can accept favours, but not the senior in a secondary school, if he wants to remain in his peer group. Staff and pupils therefore establish a reciprocal relationship differing between schools, but always characterized by norms on both sides inhibiting close, equal contacts.

The norms governing their relations with teachers are felt by pupils as pressures to accept a subordinate, restrained status. 'The classroom situation is, from the pupil's point of view especially, a social situation which is dominated by an authority figure.'[17] Thus the clue to the relation between the status of staff and pupils is the maintenance of social distance. The culture of the school lays down guide-lines which may define this as wide and formal, or warm and close, but it is always there, enabling staff to maintain their authority and pupils to maintain their independence. The teaching role is a quadrille, requiring close relations for efficient learning, but

c

distance for the security of both parties. This delicate balance is sustained by rapid return to formality the moment pupils begin to get familiar, or if staff begin to get too personal. The statuses of headteacher, staff and pupil are clearly defined within the culture of the school and the education system as a whole.

Other administrative statuses such as school secretary, cleaners, catering staff are less clearly defined. The most interesting is the school caretaker. His duties are specific and can be determined rigidly. Unlike the staff he has a definite field of competence. This enables him to dictate to staff who want to carry out non-routine activities. The range of these activities clashes with his specific obligations. In one case the headteacher was lent a ladder for Christmas decorating, but had to carry it to the school hall himself as the caretaker did not see this as his job. His status is neutral, not involved with staff or pupils as persons to whom obligations are felt. He can be ruthlessly impartial in refusing a teacher a room after school, because he is not involved in the staffroom, but his power is often increased by his direct contact with the headteacher. Frequently he will share communications which are not available to the rest of the staff. His independent status gives him power in excess of official definition.

This explains the unique position of many caretakers. In infant schools they can become father figures, but with older children this changes to a more aggressive role. His rights and obligations are not defined by the same criteria as school teaching staff. Similarly, the caretaker is not bound by the same affective relations with the children that are necessary for the teachers. To him the children are makers of work and enemies of cleanliness. Consequently, aided by his access to the headteacher, without being bound by professional ethics, he can be very ruthless. Indeed, some schools only seem to run by his permission. He is often an important agent in keeping order. Children can play around with a teacher, but when the caretaker says get out, they move quickly. His language and his actions need be less restrained. Similarly, a school secretary or catering manageress can become key figures in a school because their status is not defined by the same norms that bind staff and pupils.

Arrangements for organizing social relations occur within school buildings. The layout of a school and its classrooms tends to symbolize the social structure and be designed for it. The traditional design gives each teacher a room in which he has autonomy. It gives the staff privacy, but places the staffroom strategically. The head's study is near the front entrance or at a focal point of the school. At one extreme were the designs of Jeremy Bentham, maximizing the control of the staff over the school through a design similar to a prison. At the other are new primary schools, without formrooms or formal layout, with spaces in which children can work, rest and play, or find privacy if required.

This difference is very significant. Primary education has broken free from the formal transmission of information from staff to pupils, and requires space for free activity, painting, resting, dancing, exploring and discussing. Primary school design therefore tends to be flexible and without closed formrooms and ranks of desks.[18] The latest designs such as Finmere, Oxfordshire (1958) or Rolls Road, Camberwell (1966), 'exploded the classroom box' to facilitate 'the pervasive flow of work and play'. Only for the nine-year-olds is there a return to an enclosed classroom. This change has been described in a progressive primary school as follows:

In the classroom the desks are probably grouped together so that the children no longer sit in serried ranks facing the teacher. Arranged in groups they can see each other, work together, discuss problems and give each other help. Status competition has given way to cooperation, and the children are learning to work as social beings, understanding and making allowances for differences in behaviour and intellect. At times the children are free to move about the classroom in following their learning activities. They leave the room for the same reasons and often take their work with them for long periods.[19]

This contrasts with this description of a class of twelve–year-olds.

They sit in desks usually, often in rows, all facing one way, although contemporary furniture and classroom organization is tending to change this. This basic grid of rows and aisles helps to define the area of attention somewhat and enables the teacher placed at the front of the class and usually with a somewhat higher desk, possibly a dais, to supervise the class and when necessary to become the focus of attention.[20]

Classrooms, then, symbolize and give meaning to the relation between staff and pupils. Lack of social distance is accompanied by an absence of physical separation. Children do not see teachers as neutral 'chalkers-and-talkers' once the layout does not symbolize this by placing them in rows facing the teacher and the blackboard. Indeed, modern infant schools do not have blackboards. In secondary school this focus persists, so that communication can flow easily to the class from the teacher, but not so easily to him or between the pupils. The formal layout reinforces the cultural definition of the situation as authoritarian. Significantly the Newsom and Schools Council Reports on facilities for older pupils, once the school-leaving age is raised, recommend new physical layouts to match the treatment of this group in a more adult way.[21]

When popular education started to develop in the late eighteenth and early nineteenth centuries, it was conceived as a way of giving elementary knowledge and moral discipline to the masses. The monitorial school, with its hierarchy of teacher, monitors and pupils in a room, was essentially a one-way transmission requiring a central, visible position for the teacher from whom instruction flowed. This has persisted although classes have got smaller and monitors have been dispensed with. The teacher has to establish his authority in the classroom. The safest way to do this is to make the layout reflect the required distance between teacher and class. The infant class has complete informality because no social distance is required. The junior class alternates from formal to informal. The secondary class rarely moves from the traditional pattern.

This relation between buildings, definition of social relations, the authority of the teacher and teaching methods, accounts for the resistance to new methods. These may be opposed as inefficient, but they also threaten the authority of the teacher by disturbing those physical arrangements which define the situation as one of submission and dominance. Student teachers practising in a very formal school, reorganize a class into groups at their peril, for they may be disturbing the relation which guarantees their acceptance as the person in charge. Moreover, lessons where children are active need more preparation and are more exhausting physically and mentally.[22]

The activities outside the classroom are also affected by building and playing space. Obviously a city school with only an asphalt strip for a playground will be unable to run a range of sports and games. But activity depends on initiative rather than facilities, and the most lavishly equipped school can be dead after four o'clock. Generally, large schools provide a greater range of opportunities, but each child tends to be less involved.[23] The small school may have fewer clubs and societies and play fewer games, but each pupil is involved in many more of these than in larger schools. The large school can leave many unnoticed, uninvolved, although it has better facilities. The remedy is often to break a large school up into houses, autonomous for activities not on the timetable, so that children can be part of a group small enough for them to be known and needed.

What goes on in a school, however, is never dictated by facilities; bright ideas can find a graveyard in the finest architecture. On the other hand, Sybil Marshall's school

. . . was the ugliest building in the place, and even that was mellowed by a hundred years of wear and tear, and by the ivy which covered a host of architectural and structural defects. . . . It was made up of one room thirty foot long and fifteen foot wide and two long porches, one at each end. There was a piano; two old, high, narrow cupboards house everything the school possessed and the doors would not close because they were warped out of shape in every direction. The desks were dual desks, shod with iron, except for one or two in which real 'infants' sat, and they were of a still earlier period, being the long, narrow type at which six babies could sit in a cramped row.[24]

Nevertheless this school was to come alive under an inspired teacher.

To summarize, a school can be seen as a network of positions or statuses to which staff and pupils are allocated and in which they learn the norms which define their roles. These stem from the formal school structure or from subcultures within it. Whatever the combination of influences, the roles are predictable and regular. This allocation and the exposure to norms determining individual behaviour has profound effects on those concerned as they play their roles. But this learning of the role is also part of the social structure, for it cannot be left to chance. This is considered in the next chapter. The effect on staff and pupils of the influence of often conflicting values and norms, due to the variety of groups to which they belong, will be the the subject of Chapter 5.

4

Socialization and social control

The allocation of persons to statuses in the social structure must be accompanied by learning the appropriate roles. But role performance must not only be learnt, it must be felt to be right, efficient and rewarding, for individual satisfaction and group solidarity. While such feelings develop naturally as a role is played, the social structure must reinforce learning by rewards and punishments. This motivation to play roles as defined within the culture is the process of socialization. Its most dramatic instance is the parents' manipulation of rewards and constraints in the satisfaction of the new-born child's biological needs to produce a social being. Similarly a school must arrange its motivations to ensure that life within it proceeds smoothly. These arrangements are crucial to the structural-functional theory of sociology with its focus on the way the parts or structures function to sustain the whole.

In a school, this socialization consists of:

1. Clear definition of appropriate behaviour.
2. Rewards for culturally appropriate behaviour.
3. Punishments to eliminate behaviour which is inappropriate.
4. Maximum exposure to the new culture.

These four features provide a continuous set of influences for learning correct behaviour in the roles. At each transition from class to class, or school to school, these sticks and carrots are used to ensure that the new role performance is learnt. For new staff as well as children, the statuses or roles must be clearly defined. There must be a clear picture of the new values and norms, and these must be shown in action by the provision of models to copy. There must be a vision of the privileges which will result from adopting the new

role. The building, formrooms, uniforms, routines, personal relations must all help the individual to see himself in his new status,
and simultaneously feel pressures which reward correct, and punish
wrong behaviour.

Professional training means that there has been a long period over
which staff can learn the role. This training frequently gives experience of more than one type of school. Within three years, mistakes can be made and forgotten as teaching practice periods are
short and in different schools. Successful performance not only has
its own intrinsic rewards, but results in praise from supervisors and
the reward of a Certificate in Education. The probationary year extends this supervised learning period at least in theory, and should
include opportunities for support from the school and inspectorate.

Professional training also helps to establish an identity with teaching as a career, which in turn results in the correct role behaviour
becoming part of the person's normal behaviour. Colleges of education provide three years among other prospective teachers in which
official activity, informal discussion and continuous assessments
concentrate the student's attention on teaching in theory and practice. The other avenue into teaching through a degree, taken in a
university, provides the subject specialists, mainly for secondary
schools. Here, postgraduate training can provide a less extensive
professional introduction, but has the same result in reinforcing the
original choice of teaching by mixing with others who have made
the same choice in an environment geared to stimulate appropriate
attitudes. Professional training, therefore, not only provides the experience, background and techniques for the teacher, but has the
unintended effect of reinforcing identification with the career.

When a new teacher arrives at his school he has to learn the local
variations in the role. A copy of the syllabus enables preparation to
be made. A visit to the school can give knowledge of facilities, but
as this is usually in the vacation it does not give an idea of the
school at work. Headteachers can help by providing advance information although examination of the probationary year shows
that this is frequently neglected.[1] The existence of a clearly defined
status, however, eases the path for the newcomer. Children are used
to granting teachers certain rights and expect others in return. The

newcomer fits into a routinized situation sustained by the pupils. They will frequently run the class without guidance, and the role he has to perform to fit into this routine can be gauged from their behaviour towards him. In the first few hours in a new school, many teachers bring prepared exercises for the children so that they can settle down to work while the teacher gets his bearings. Simple, repetitive work is found in all schools and can serve to gain time to observe the routine in the new situation.

The socialization of the school child

Children face a succession of new statuses as they pass through school. At each stage there is a situation organized to teach the new behaviour. Probably the most drastic transition occurs when the child first arrives at school, particularly when there has been no previous attendance at a play centre or nursery class. A variety of methods is adopted at this stage. The reception class is arranged to give a relaxed, informal atmosphere, with the teaching settling the children into school routine gradually and with careful attention to the needs of individuals. Mothers can be invited to spend time with their children in the class before entry. The intakes can be staggered to make sure that reception classes are small and that newcomers are assimilated into an already functioning group. Others take children into an established class and appoint another infant to look after each new child.

Nevertheless, the door has still to be shut sometimes to stop some children rushing after their departing mothers. In one study, 65 per cent were reluctant to go to school at some time in their first year in the infants.[2] The need for close personal attachments is reduced by gently admonishing excessive claims on the time of the teacher. The children are praised for behaving like big boys and girls, for giving up childish habits. Selfish or disruptive behaviour is corrected and cooperative play in groups practised. But the classes are still organized to give a maximum of security for the children. Some infant schools use vertical, all-age or family grouping, whereby a child remains in the same class, with the same teacher, for all his time in the school. It is claimed that this system 'gives to the children a valuable sense of security and stability, and to their teacher a deeper quality of insight into their all-round development and character which springs from 2 or 3 years of close and intimate association'.[3] Family grouping is practised in a minority of schools. More common is promotion by age or progress in learning to read. Movement from class to class is frequently arranged each term to match the termly admissions. To avoid this disturbance to a stable relation between child and teacher, the Plowden Committee recommended that there should only be one intake every year.[4] But this change was only to be made after part-time nursery education had been made available for all who wished it, so that the children would be prepared for full-time schooling.

The infant and junior classes tend to get progressively more formal in structure. This not only mirrors the more formal nature of work, but eventually prepares children for transition to secondary school. This is most apparent in the top junior form, which in areas of selective secondary education can be very formal and academic. This is frequently the class taken by the headteacher or a senior member of the male staff. But the trend is continuous from the arrival at seven from the infants. The time taken on an activity is increased until formal lessons become common. Movement around the classroom is restrained in preparation for the time when permission will be required for leaving a desk. Children are no longer allowed to go to the toilet at will. The teacher steadily increases the demands for high standards and consistent effort. For good or bad, the activity of the junior school becomes the restraint of the secondary.

Not only is the transfer at eleven years to a new school, but secondary schools tend to be larger, organized more formally and have relationships that are neutral. Reluctance to go to school reappears. The pupils are increasingly judged on performance rather than as persons. Surnames replace Christian names for the boys, desks rarely deviate from their columns and rows, and all the time there are hundreds of older adolescents dictating the pace of life. From the top of the juniors the child goes to the bottom of the secondary school. Work is geared more rigidly to a syllabus and examinations are taken regularly. This can be summed up as an increasing emphasis on instrumental activity. The grammar school tends to be farthest along this road, but in all schools instrumental action increases shortly before leaving, when education is usually seen as a means to ends external to the school, rather than focusing on the needs and values of the children. Expressive activity is reduced and moral action is given a lower priority.

Secondary schools structure the life of first-year pupils to accelerate the role learning; some see this as 'breaking them in'.[5] The need to forget childish ways is stressed: children are encouraged to wear school uniform, there is to be no more going to the toilet at odd times, only between lessons or at break. Textbooks are now kept by the children, to be bound and kept clean. Bringing pets and toys to school is stopped. Above all children no longer have the security of their permanent teacher and classroom. Now they circulate between different teachers and rooms as subjects increasingly become more specialized. Their contacts with specialist teachers tend to be brief and impersonal. Some schools soften the strains of transfer by visits before entry or talks by secondary school teachers in the primary schools. Some take in new pupils a day before the rest.[6] Some have form teachers responsible for teaching two or more subjects in their first years.

However painful some children find the transition from class to class or school to school, the learning period is usually short. Within a short time the class has established a normative structure in which individual children can feel secure because they know what is expected of them by their peers and by the teachers. The behaviour of a new pupil who arrives after the rest illustrates how tightly integrated a school class can become, and how firmly norms become established. The class view the newcomer with suspicion. It takes time for him to be accepted. Meanwhile he has to learn who's who and what's what. He makes mistakes, upsets people and often becomes over demonstrative or withdrawn as a reaction to his awkward, marginal status.

Each movement up the school is marked with new privileges and obligations. School caps are replaced by scarves, coffee replaces milk at break time, seniors are allowed to play in the gym at lunchtime or join clubs after school. The sixth form in a grammar school, or a fifth form in a secondary modern school, is allowed to use their form-rooms as common rooms, or are given a room for this purpose. Sometimes they are waited on at table or have a special dining area. Some are made prefects, involving them in new rights and obligations to match this new status. But again this usually follows preparation for the role as monitors or form prefects, lower down the school.

Preparation for such changes of status frequently occurs in advance. When the prospects of promotion become apparent there is an assumption of the characteristics of the future role. The potential senior mistress looking for promotion adopts an air of authority and associates more with the headteacher. The future prefect stops playing with the toughs and models his behaviour on the more dignified seniors. This is the process of anticipatory socialization. It is accompanied by a change of reference group. The group whose behaviour is taken as a model changes from present company to those who will be the new colleagues. The actual promotion is therefore often partly a consequence of the individual anticipating it, and changing his behaviour accordingly. He is then seen as a potential headmaster or prefect. Students arriving at colleges of education have often already adopted many of the social and professional aspects of teaching. They tend to dress conservatively, behave moderately, and are less prone to excessive 'rag' behaviour than other students. They use their own experience in the classroom to build up an image of themselves as teachers so that first performance is often highly professional.

Schools and colleges are therefore structured to ensure adequate learning of the roles that go with positions in their division of labour. This process of socialization is continuous throughout education. Each stage prepares for the next and breaks the behaviour patterns associated with the stage before. From the infants to the secondary school there is a progressive elimination of unstructured situations. As social distance between staff and pupils is widened, ambiguous situations are redefined to reduce possible stress. The formality of the secondary school results in little strain because the rules and routines tell staff and pupils what is expected of them. The norms therefore bring security which can no longer

come from close personal contacts. Etiquette eases the friction between staff and pupils once their knowledge of each other as persons
is limited.

In the introduction to Chapter 2, the sociologist was compared
with the entomologist. But men are not insects. They do not respond
instinctively. However powerful the social pressures on individuals,
they can still act in disruptive, rebellious ways. Socialization is
never strong enough to produce individuals perfectly tailored to fit
into the social structure, even with an adequate system there will
never be completely harmonious relations nor complete consensus
over values. Individuals do not perform roles as robots, they interpret them and modify their behaviour in ways that can upset or
change the working of the system.

They are often encouraged in this by outside influences, in their
family life or among their friends. However many revisions of the
system are made to ensure a fair deal for the working class child,
whether by getting rid of selection or streaming, or altering conditions and curriculum, children will still arrive at school with different motivations. What happens in school is influenced by attitudes learned by the children outside. The way they use the chance
offered is probably developed very early. Jones, examining samples
of working class and middle class mothers, showed that the latter
prepared their under fives better for school.[7] This was not only for
academic work, but they taught their children to be more active in
their learning so that they would get the most out of their education.
Further, they saw no difference between their job as mothers, and
that of the teacher as educator. They were partners in the education
of the same child. The working class mothers did less preparation,
saw the pupil's role as passive and saw the teacher as doing a job
unrelated to theirs as mothers. Even at this stage, before five years
old, the children were being motivated differently. The utilization of
talent may be more a matter of propaganda directed at mothers of
young children, than alterations in the structure of the school
system. Indeed, work at the Centre for the Study of Human Development in London University has shown that the environment
has an effect on a child's potential to benefit from education before
he reaches school.[8] No differences between groups of children from

different social classes were measurable at eighteen months, but at five years old, the children of middle class parents had gained fifteen Intelligence Quotient points, while the children of semi-skilled and unskilled workers had lost about ten points.

Deviations

The model of the school used so far has not included many tensions that are, in reality, inevitable. Now it will be extended, using the work of R. K. Merton, himself developing ideas of E. Durkheim.[9] The structure of norms in society, particularly in conditions of rapid change, tends to break down. People find that the old ways are no guide to how to behave in a new situation. Individual life in urban industrial society is not usually tightly regulated and moral pressures are sometimes weak. Durkheim called the completely norm-less state anomy. More common is the situation where means (norms) do not match ends (values). Individuals perceive and are motivated by cultural values, but find that they have no way of reaching these goals in a legitimate way.

This is frequently the case in a school. Railway Cuttings Secondary Modern School may adopt the motto 'Manners maketh man', but its staff fight a losing battle to preserve gentility. School C, in Chapter 3, aimed to give everyone some form of examination qualification, but inevitably failed. Staff and pupils opt out of the race once they see there is no point in trying. Others find greater satisfactions outside the school and look forward to getting ahead in life without its help or reconcile themselves to a low status. These individuals not sharing the values of the school are alienated. In the studies by Lacey and Hargreaves, streaming resulted in the alienation of the lower streams.[10] Schools then have a tendency to anomy, manifested in a failure to contain pupils within their norms. In extreme cases the moral or normative order of a school can collapse and individual conduct becomes unregulated.

Individual adaptation of roles occurs whenever legitimate means and ends get out of step. Consequently, the following patterns occur frequently in schools. The conformist approaches perfect socialization. He accepts the goals of the school and works zealously to attain them, usually sitting in the front row of his class. Others accept the goals but not the means. They are innovators, always after new methods of doing the work, new ways of reaching the top. Sometimes this will involve some form of cheating, working the system, ploys whereby illegal means are adopted, to achieve the goals. Indeed, the stress on achieving good examination results asks for such short-circuiting both from staff and pupils. The teacher gives out skeleton answers to predicted questions and deviates in the same way as the pupil who sneaks useful data on a sheet of blotting paper to an examination.

Other forms of non-conformity involve a rejection of the cultural goals and values. Such persons are alienated. The ritualist loses sight of the goals and goes through the motions compulsively, but with little aim. He is the child who works very hard but without direction, the teacher who has sunk into a rut. Both carry on into a routine, without reference to where they are going. This is probably most common among school staffs, for the repetition of lessons, a routine geared to children, can dull the sense of mission until the purposes of education are lost to sight.

Finally, there are forms of adaptation in which goals and means are rejected together. These rarely apply to teachers who will have left the profession prior to taking up such a position. The retreatist opts out, dissociates himself from the school system. Some children lose all interest in school. They form a passive minority, usually sitting in the back row. They are rarely serious trouble-makers, but are disinterested, untidy, sullen, time-servers waiting to leave. Occasionally a staffroom contains a teacher who has withdrawn into his subject and has forgotten his role as teacher. This can degenerate into passionate, scholastic excursions into obscure academic by-ways, which pass over the form, who amuse themselves as best they can. Even headmasters can adopt such a retreatist position:

The headmaster was nowhere to be seen. He was shut up in his study, it seemed: the general belief of the staff was that he was hiding under the table. Perhaps this was exaggerating and that he really had some important clerical work to attend to. But I'm sure that it was with no reluctance that he handed over to the senior master the responsibility of opening the school gates and allowing the wild mob to surge into the playground. He made one fleeting appearance with some lists in his hand, surveyed the indisciplined rabble with an anxious eye, then thrust the lists into the senior master's hand and departed. It was a significant, almost a symbolic action.[11]

More troublesome are the rebels, not only alienated from means and ends, but trying to change them. Some children reject the values of school and the rules which embody them. Given support from a group, their progress from infant to school leaver is the teacher's burden.

These adaptations account for change in the social system, for each offers an alternative set of norms and values and may give rise to a group trying to change things; each is indicative of a lack of consensus, a split in the normative structure. This analysis by Merton of individual adaptations, shows how social structures can generate deviant as well as conformist behaviour, extends structural-functional theory to show how change occurs and in a system seen in equilibrium, although the model is still too utopian to provide a complete picture of an organization like a school.

These adaptations can be seen as a failure in the socialization process, due to inconsistencies in the relation between values and norms. But a second set of deviations can occur because the learning of one role conflicts with another. This results from the same individual playing roles in different organizations. The teacher is also a husband, wife, parent, voter, sportsman and so on. These statuses may involve him in contradictory demands. He may be an atheist, yet be expected to take part in a compulsory act of worship, or even be asked to take Religious Education. His conscience and ambition conflict. Should he forget the former and gain favour, or refuse to conform and spoil his chances of promotion? The married woman teacher has obligations to her family and to the school. Should she stay at home when her child is ill and let her colleagues down, or get someone to look after the child for her?

These are cases of role conflict or strain. They occur whenever individuals are involved in different organizations and institutions. They occur among children when the demands of the school conflict with those outside. The working class boy who arrives at grammar school may find its codes of behaviour, homework, uniform, ridiculed by friends who have gone to secondary modern or technical schools. When they leave school at an earlier age he contrasts their affluent independence with his status as pupil. Schools as cultural hothouses necessarily create role strains as part of their job of socializing the young into adults. School values are always more elevated than those common outside them. Some children reject the school's culture because the costs are too high, particularly when there is no attempt to adjust it for older pupils.

These strains are inevitable once individuals are involved in specialist organizations in complex societies. Schools are one such organization and are usually the first opportunity for young children, previously playing parts only in their family, and in their neighbourhood, to experience role strain. The parent who pushes the child to read and write, while the school sees this as undesirable and delays applying pressure; the mother who dresses her child badly in a school where standards are very high; these are placing the child in a position where choice is between irreconcilable alternatives.

Social control

Anomy and role strain can both result in some children and staff not fitting into a school. An absence or disarray of norms presents a situation calling for tough corrective measures. Where different role prescriptions clash, official pressure can only increase the strain, even though it may result in the individual giving up the unofficial role. But roles may not be performed correctly because the learning process has been inefficient or absent. Here socialization has failed. Nevertheless, behaviour must still be controlled. There are mechanisms for eliminating stresses which can trigger off deviance and also check on behaviour before it can threaten social order. Controls on behaviour operate for all statuses and at both informal and formal levels. They are built into the social structure, like stabilizers on an ocean liner. They can range from the trivial to the severe, from an annoyed glance to ritual expulsion from the school. They

are built into the structure, felt by staff and pupils as soon as behaviour strays from the straight and narrow.

The regulation of behaviour will be discussed in Chapter 7. Here
the focus will not be on the way that sticks and carrots ensure that
roles are performed, but rather on the way that stresses are avoided
and reduced. The child who monopolizes the teacher's time in the
junior school is discouraged by the teacher as subtly as possible,
but is also subject to derision by the class. The chatterer in an
obedient class is silenced by looks and comments as well as being
silenced by the teacher's threats or actions. The creep, the sneak or
the tell-tale is dealt with in the playground. Teachers manipulate
this by making the class responsible for the behaviour of individuals.
The boy who keeps talking and stops the form going out to play is
made very aware that he is responsible. Conversely, approved
behaviour is rewarded through rewarding the class.

Similarly teachers are subject to social controls. The over-pro-
gressive are reminded that the noise in their classroom is disturbing
others. The clock-watcher is reminded that he is not pulling his
weight. The extremely punitive teacher is ostracized. Similarly the
teacher who is too familiar with the children is corrected by their
withdrawal from contact and the hostility of the staff. Favouritism
is corrected by the hostile attitude of the majority. Meanwhile,
appropriate role-performance is rewarded officially and unofficially
by promotion, allowances and the favourable attitude of the staff
and pupils. These sanctions form a pattern of predictable responses.
They are part of the definition of the situation. But controls must
also prevent stress. In a utopia, there would be harmonious relations
and therefore no deviants and no need for social controls. Angels
need no correcting. There are therefore some mechanisms in all
social systems reducing stresses, or insulating those areas where
these are most likely to happen, to avoid the flare-up of conflict.

These areas where tension is high because people meet with different definitions of the situation, or meet before they can adjust
to the other party, are frequent where private life becomes public,
where informal meets formal and unofficial the official. An actor
walking on to the stage, a waitress leaving the kitchen to enter the
restaurant, a child entering a classroom, all are passing from a world

in which behaviour can be natural among friends to one in which it must be formal among strangers. Goffman has called these back region and front region, or backstage and onstage.[12] It is at these points that underlying differences often emerge when the switch in behaviour is not quick enough. The actor is seen laughing before entering as a mourner, the waitress stops pushing food around with her fingers just too late and the child swallows his sweet just after the teacher has spotted it.

Pupils in informal groups in the playground, in unsupervised classrooms, in toilets, behind convenient sheds, while staff relax in their common room, can be little devils. But when staff and pupils are in contact, each will play their official roles, put on their best behaviour, and practise 'impression management'.[13] This putting on an act exists whenever staff and pupils meet. Occasionally *faux pas* are made, clangers dropped. Children go on talking without realizing that the teacher has returned. A member of staff might be undiplomatic enough to look behind the gym. Staff don't notice the head has come into their common room. Normally the switch in behaviour is instantaneous: a teacher changes from being a relaxed, bawdy colleague to being an aloof, puritan autocrat as he opens the staffroom door to answer a knock from a child who simultaneously changes from a grinning urchin bent on disturbing the staff's midday leisure, to a plaintive sufferer from a headache.

The threat of mistakes leads to these danger points being insulated. At break and dinner-time, staff and pupils are segregated to avoid excessive off-duty contact. Children must only knock on the staffroom door in emergencies and must always wait for the door to be opened. Staff don't pry too conscientiously into the hidden parts of the toilets or playground. Whenever situations are not well defined as official or unofficial, insulating processes occur. Staff seek some privacy at school meals, while those on duty adopt an uneasy compromise between classroom and playground discipline. The last days of term are detached from normal routine so that restlessness is not taken as a permanent loosening of discipline.

These social controls point to an important aspect of the social structure of a school. While statuses are clearly defined, role performance raises little stress. But at those points where the definition is confused there is a possibility of tension. The tendency to drop formal arrangements and methods has tended to confuse definitions. Role conflicts therefore are not only due to incompatible demands in the organization, but to defects in the social structure. Staff and pupils feel easier when onstage behaviour and front region are known to everyone and enforced. This comes back to the definition of the situation which is therefore necessary, not only for communication and interaction but for individual security. Resistance to new methods, while rationalized in intellectual argument, is often a hidden defence against exposing the delicate area.

Manners and etiquette serve to protect other sources of possible deviance. The new teacher calls the headmaster 'Sir' because this is safe. Later he may get on to Christian name terms, but he can't afford to make a mistake at the beginning, so he uses the formal approach. Classes, uncertain whether a new teacher is Miss or Mrs, refer to her as 'Miss'. They stand up when strangers enter, raise their hands to get attention, knock and wait outside a strange class-room. As time brings familiarity with the norms, this formality can be relaxed without embarrassment or friction.

However effective the forestalling mechanisms, some stress is inevitable. There must therefore be ways in which this can be dissipated without disrupting the whole system. The most common device is to provide safety valves, whereby behaviour which is usually illegal is allowed by channelling it into lawful outlets. A teacher must be a Dr Jekyll in the classroom but can become a Mr Hyde in the staffroom. School clubs and societies allow children to pursue interests outside the curriculum, but they also enable staff to get closer to children than is sanctioned in the classroom. Physical education dissipates energy that could destroy class control. A quick rush round the playground can save a double period from breaking up. Break and dinner-time refresh staff and pupils. Infants and juniors may have several short breaks during the day. Holidays are long and refreshing, and release built-up tensions for the staff.

The younger the children, the more common are such devices. Infant classes have short sessions at a variety of activities. The length of each will be varied by the teacher according to the state of the children. If necessary she will make a class rest their heads on the desks or sit them on the floor and tell a story. New infant schools have bunks for resting. Their day is shorter, being length- ened as ability to concentrate increases with age. At the top of the secondary school, steam is let off by arranging for record-playing and dancing at lunchtime for senior pupils, by allowing them to use their formroom as a club, or by giving them special accommoda- tion. The Schools' Council report on raising the school-leaving age, following up the recommendations of the Newsom Committee, stresses the need for staff–pupil relations to be the same in the class- room as in the corridor or in extra-curricular activity, to ensure that the sixteen-year-old is treated as an adult. When the pupil becomes a student in a college the tension is dissipated more frequently in the lecture room itself, as the lecturer can afford to reduce the distance between himself and his group without fear of any loss of authority.

Above all, the school must provide outlets for as wide a variety of tastes as possible. The un-athletic must not be frustrated by over- emphasis on games, or the non-academic surrounded by rewards for examination success alone. The artistic child must be allowed an outlet as well as those interested in muscle-building. The provision of a variety of outlets reduces frustration and the amount of deviance. But these outlets must still be organized by the school, part of the total pattern of social control. In all areas the school develops these outlets, usually without deliberate analysis of need, but the latent function is to increase social control by reducing deviance from the norms.

A school, then, can be viewed as a social structure, consisting of statuses, rather like the atoms in a molecular model. Between these statuses are regular patterns of behaviour or roles. The structure tends to persist while different individuals fill these positions. Staff and pupils come and go, but the school as a social organization con- tinues relatively unchanged. While individual interpretations of the role occur, these are limited not only by the individual making the role his own, once he is placed in the status, but by the social con- trols which limit the motivation to deviate.

Part 3

A conflict model of the school

5

Schools as centres of conflict

The existence of individuals who deviate from norms, and the tendency for such deviation to result from inconsistencies in the social structure of the school, or between the school and other agencies of socialization, suggest that the simple structural-functional model used so far is incomplete. Adaptations in the performance of roles to meet inconsistent demands mean that social organizations in equilibrium will be rare. Continual change is likely to occur as individuals adapt to influences both within the institution and from outside. But even this extension is inadequate when applied to such organizations as schools. Individuals rarely adopt deviant roles in isolation. Innovators and rebels become leaders of groups pressing for change, opposing authority and resisting official influences. Ritualists and retreatists form withdrawn minorities. In both cases, whether active or passive, groups form and develop their own subculture, frequently clashing among themselves and with the dominant group.

This tendency for individual deviance to obtain social support, to become 'one of the boys', has appeared so far in the division between the formal and the informal, official and unofficial, onstage and backstage areas of school life. Teachers usually work on the principle of divide and rule, isolating the trouble-maker by punishing the class for his bad behaviour or by arranging the formroom to break up his clique. This is successful but builds up tensions which remain when the teachers are out of sight.[1] Backstage the 'persecuted' may be more popular than ever, and once driven underground detection and remedy become more difficult. This is the first major flaw in the structural-functional model. All organizations contain groups that are in conflict, not harmony. If goals are to be achieved, these opposition groups must be forced to toe the official line.

Coercion as well as consensus are present, therefore, provided the observer looks deep enough. A state of continuous change, persistent conflicts and the use of force to achieve official goals, are conditions necessitating a new theory based on conflict rather than harmony. This is a second major model used in contemporary sociology. It is applicable to all schools, from the genteel to those containing the roaring boys and young devils.

It would be surprising to find any organization in which there was no clash of interest between groups. The allocation of persons to different statuses means that the organization is viewed with different perspective. Each person learns those parts of the culture which apply to his status. None sees the whole picture, formal and informal. Individuals sharing the same status in the same social structure, having the same view of the whole, will tend to develop common interests which are different from those of other status groups. Even a spontaneous association of friends to play games will experience conflict as soon as a captain, secretary or committee is appointed, for immediately these will see things differently from the rank and file. Manufacturers and consumers, officers and ranks, managers and workers, governors and governed will all have conflicting interests and will try to achieve different goals within the organization.

In a school, pupils and staff will see the same things in different lights. They will come to school from different backgrounds, with different tastes, experiences and prospects, and will want to satisfy different needs. Inevitably staff will exercise their power to ensure that they get their way, but this often means overcoming the resistance of the children. An official, adult culture will exert power over groups of pupils with different values. 'I could have worked harder but what's the use if you don't get any encouragement.' 'We had the feeling that if they treated us like children, we'd behave like it.' 'They couldn't control us because they treated us like children.' These quotations from the Newsom Report illustrate more moderate antagonisms.[2] The hostility may be articulated only among older children, but its origins lie in the early years of school life. The conflict increases as pupils get older and receive greater support for hostile attitudes from outside the school, but it is present at all ages. Going to school is itself a restriction on liberty and the routine within it is continually restraining the natural desires of the pupils. 'Although some yearned for the days that were gone, very many more were glad to have left these times behind. School is all very well for children, but when you are older you want something more.'[3] However well the children are involved they must be checked at times and many will always creep like snails, unwillingly to school and form a resistance movement within it. Teaching is partly designed to keep such resistance under control. The exhaustion of teachers at the end of the school day is due to the constant strain of organizing the timetable to ensure that latent stress does not overflow into actual disorder.

Schools in the slums tend to be particularly wearing because they are often badly equipped and very old. In 1963, 79 per cent of secondary schools in these areas were described as seriously inadequate.[4] The Plowden Committee reported a similar situation in primary schools in 1967.[5] Many of the children come from homes and neighbourhoods with values which contradict those of the school and in which violence may be normal. The rate of attendance is low and few stay beyond the minimum leaving age. Waller in *The Sociology of Teaching* saw schools in this light.[6]

To understand the political structure of the school we must know that the school is organized on the authority principle and that that authority is constantly threatened. . . . There is a constant interaction between the elements of the authoritative system; the school is continually threatened because it is autocratic, and it has to be autocratic because it is threatened. The antagonistic forces are balanced in that ever fickle equilibrium which is discipline.

It is significant that Waller's book was written before the development of theories on which much of the analysis in preceding chapters was based. It is honest in not fitting observed facts into a theory. However, it probably underestimated the strength of normative pressures in the school and the ability of teachers to use this to ensure compliance. This is discussed in Chapter 7.

Another aspect of school structure also leads to conflict. The motivations available for children can be instrumental, the view of a brighter future as a reward for hard work, or expressive, the immediate satisfaction of emotional needs. Neither can be totally effective in the normal school. With teacher-pupil ratios of one to thirty, forty or even fifty, the dull and slow are often sacrificed in the quest of academic or athletic success. The teacher cannot arrange for all to succeed, although the lack of reward for many remains a major weakness in teaching. Similarly one teacher cannot ensure that the needs of all the class are met. Some individuals will become retreatists or rebels once the initial promise of the informal, play-centred infant class develops into the more rigid discipline of the junior school.

Schools frequently aggravate this by stressing goals which can be achieved only by a few. Only a minority in the junior school will get a grammar school place, and a majority in the secondary modern school will not take G.C.E. or C.S.E. Further, teachers tend to concentrate their efforts on the few, because they are the most rewarding and the easiest to work with; they receive the attention, the praise and the prizes. At the back of every primary school class are children who will spend ten years without much achievement or attention. They consolidate into groups which seek satisfaction through informal activity, and which oppose school policy and disrupt its working. This disruption takes the form of a wearing series of minor interruptions. Books are left behind, pencils mislaid, pens are empty and the class arrives late. Once it is ready to start, a series of irrelevant questions, each just sensible enough to require answering, causes more delay. The silence of work is marred by nudging, laughing, remarks just loud enough to be heard. The teacher is continually on the brink of making each an issue, but none is sufficiently serious by itself.

The art of playing up in class is one that has been practised for generations, yet today there is more of this sort of thing than would have been tolerated years ago. The awkward boy is a case apart, and indeed, requires a chapter to himself, but there is a wide group of boys who are not really delinquent or unpleasant, who are always ready to join in any 'playing up' sessions.[7]

The very existence of school is a limit on freedom and the clashes of interest will occur even in the most progressive. 'We have always maintained that human beings, both young and old, should be free in what they think, believe and say, but not necessarily in what they do. The freedom in which we strongly believe is not freedom from physical restriction but freedom of mind and spirit.'[8] This principle, expressed by the Headmaster of Frensham Heights School in reply to a description of it as a 'do as you want' school, honestly illustrates the limits of freedom and the consequent clash of interests and the need for coercion.

Progressive school managements regard it as essential to mental health that regulation should be minimal. Such conditions are most likely to be found in boarding schools, outside densely populated urban areas which are liable to promote and sustain attitudes conflicting with those of teachers. At the other pole are schools in slum areas where there is a running war against the teachers' standards. Webb[9] has described the consequent hostility in his school as follows:

Hostility (between teachers and boys) is the key feature at Black School. It is present whenever a teacher deals with boys but varies in intensity. At one extreme (uncommon but illuminating) it can be almost ferocious, when for example an inexperienced teacher wrestles with a lad for possession of a flick knife, surrounded by cheering boys. Or when a gang yell derisively at a teacher, hoping twilight in the playground will mask their identity. At the other extreme, the hostility is so mild that it needs inverted commas. An example would be a teacher trying to make a class get on with a given task. They play him up by exaggerating the bluntness, or breaking the points, of their pencils, or losing rubbers, or complaining loudly that they cannot see the blackboard, no matter where he stations it. With firmness, and not without humour, he overcomes their irrepressibility. Here the 'hostility' is like that between two football teams playing a really friendly match – on both sides there is an element of play for play's sake.[9]

However harmonious the relations are between pupils in a school, force will be used. Schools are never fully democratic, for they are never fully voluntary, nor can staff delegate real authority to pupils. There will inevitably be domination and subjection. In Waller's terms 'it is not enough to point out that the school is a despotism. It is a despotism in a state of perilous equilibrium'.[10] This applies in all organizations where interests clash but in school it is inherent in the juxtaposition of adult and child. Education is moral, concerned with transmitting 'right' values. The school is organized to surround children with moral influences to regulate behaviour. This is not just the maintenance of normal civilized behaviour, for the school tries to be a super moral agent in which actions accepted or ignored outside are actively discouraged. A teacher has to stop swearing and violence, contain children in a classroom, keep them from chatting and make them work to a timetable. These are unnatural restrictions which a child rarely experiences outside school. A teacher, therefore, is always stressing what is right and wrong. He is a moral agent and under the strain of having to sustain this through the day. A teacher has to fight against losing his temper, or excessive nagging, for this reduces his hold over his class and his impact as a model.

Definition of the situation, whereby individuals have a clear idea of their obligations and rights, is the basis of social order. Organization and policy are designed to this end. Schools are designed architecturally so that children can be continually supervised in case disorder threatens. Jeremy Bentham's design for schools, as for prisons, sought to enable a head and his staff to keep all areas under supervision. The teacher in a monitorial school sat on a platform above the class. Staffrooms and headteacher's study overlook the playground.

Similarly life is organized to contain the children within a system or order. Staff learn where and at what times disorder is likely to break out. They see the juniors into the school, making sure they are seen in the corridors and never leave the class alone in the room for any length of time. They anticipate trouble at certain times of the day and year, and organize to avoid it. They know who are the potential trouble-makers and ringleaders, and are quick to check or isolate trouble from these. Sending out of the room or to the headteacher may be discouraged, but it is doubly effective because it brings in a higher authority and also removes the spark from the tinder. Often teachers make a deliberate effort to get to know individuals or groups who can disturb the peace, and to win them over by being particularly friendly or helpful.

In addition, staff employ children to help them spread their influence and keep control. The appointment of form monitors and school prefects may prepare them for leadership, but they act as N.C.O.s in the authority structure. In the public schools prefects may wield considerable independent power, but usually their authority is legitimate only because it is backed by the power of the staff. This delegation is also accomplished by selecting a child to carry orders to others. This device is used in all schools, but is more effective among juniors. Here involvement in the school is greater and the need for coercion consequently less, and this makes delegation more effective. An eight-year-old will willingly correct his peers on instructions from a teacher and they will obey, but a fifteen-year-old will be reluctant and probably unsuccessful, unless backed by the visible power of the teacher.

However, even in the worst school, the conflict of interests and the correction of bad behaviour rarely result in violence. Conflict is rarely vicious, rather played out between staff and pupils with agreed rules. The class knows how far it can go before the teacher takes serious action. The experienced teacher ignores much mis-behaviour which is irrelevant to his definition of the situation. Only when this is threatened does he take action. There is continual give and take, adjusted to the time of the day or term, the weather and the subject being taught. As a class starts to go too far the teacher reminds them that this is 'the last time he will warn' or spells out what will happen if trouble continues. But even if he has to punish, it will be in a way which is predictable for the pupils. The punish-ment will fit the crime, the number of warnings given and the customary procedures. If he suddenly applies extremely harsh punishments, the class will be indignant, and he may later reduce the penalties (though this may be taken as a sign of weakness).

A teacher becomes adept not only at ignoring some bad behaviour but also at not seeing it. He is in a delicate situation. If he hears a child swear to another in conversation he feels he should check him. But he also knows that swearing may seem natural to the child. By checking it he makes it an issue. He can talk to the child or punish, but in one case he may seem rather narrow minded, in the other unfair. Each reduces his influence when he must correct a serious offence. Thus teachers become experts at not hearing or noticing 'backstage' casual remarks or misbehaviour. To use a military analogy, being involved in a battle they must not use up their reserves in tactical asides and spoil the overall strategy. To avoid this they define the rules of the game very subtly, granting children areas where they can be free from strict regulation, but rigidly enforcing others.

According to Smelser, hostile outbursts are most likely when the following conditions occur.[11] First, the social structure must provide the right setting. Good communication among the aggrieved, chances of expressing the grievance and a visible target on which to focus it will produce common feelings and the possibility of action. Second, there must be tension between two groups. Third, there must be some spark to set the outburst into flame.

Classrooms are ideal situations for such hostile outbursts. There are the pupils contained together over long periods of time; the teacher is continually having to frustrate them. The situation is often, in Waller's terms in 'fickle equilibrium'. An act of violence, an action by the teacher which is seen as unfair, a rebel in the class reacting sharply and supported by his friends, and the class expresses itself in an outburst of temper, even violence or destruction, either in the classroom or on school property elsewhere.

But even with all the conditions necessary for such outbursts, they are rare, even in the roughest class. The reasons for this lie in the strong normative pressure to be orderly that pervades most schools. Further, a teacher is in an ideal position to break the class up, to stop collective action, to arrange for the slow release of strain, to apply sanctions which consolidate social control before an outburst is imminent, to win over some of the class to bridge the cleavage, to keep the tension down and to ensure that no flare-up occurs. Above all, pupils and staff are linked by norms which both share and which constrain them to recognize some at least of each other's rights.

If an outburst does occur, despite the reduction, deflection and exhaustion of energy organized by the teacher, order is restored by isolating the leaders and breaking the communications in the class. A ringleader is called or hauled out. The teacher swings attention to himself to stop the pupils reinforcing each other. Teachers in charge of large numbers in the hall on a rainy day during the lunch hour carry a whistle to get attention. The teacher remains outside the trouble, visibly a symbol of authority, acting to restore order first, worrying about justice later. Often the most vulnerable is selected for immediate punishment to shock the others into order. Later the sentence is amended while the ringleaders are dealt with severely. These practices, both in building up social controls to avoid open disorder and in dealing with it once it occurs, have evolved without deliberate analysis of the situation. They have worked, therefore they are used. The reason why they work is that the class and its teacher interact within a situation defined by norms which constrain both. Symbolic action by the teacher is understood, acted on and is usually sufficient to restore order.

Conflict in schools can break out into violence, but is more likely to persist as a passive resistance. Only a small minority are likely to be openly rebellious. The Newsom Report on the education of the average and below average pupil in secondary schools, compared three different types of child.[12] Even for the most troublesome category, teachers only found 7 per cent as 'especially difficult'. But 38 per cent were 'neither cooperative nor difficult'. In this category were the children who resist passively, for whom school is a bore; who daydream the hours away, neither learning nor contributing. In research on the problems faced by teachers in the classroom, by Wickman in America and Gabriel in Britain, these apathetic cases caused little concern.[13] They were more numerous than the openly rebellious, were probably getting as little out of their education, but they could be safely left as they were not disruptive. Passivity, even withdrawal, did not seem to be a matter of much concern compared with keeping order and pushing on with the syllabus, even though this kind of behaviour may be a symptom of personality disorder.

Poor attendance records are found among both active and passive cases. The male 'Robinsons' of the Newsom Report, coming from the worst environment, having the worst record for discipline, had over five times the truancy rate of the 'Browns', the most disciplined. Female 'Robinsons' had a truancy rate three times the 'Browns' from the most favourable environment. Similarly, the 'Robinsons' were less likely to be set homework and to wear school uniform. They were not involved in the school, were poorly motivated at work and were not willingly cooperative.

The description of the school in Chapters 2, 3, and 4 has shown the strength of the pressures on pupils to conform. Open hostility to staff is difficult to maintain in the face of the internal organization of the school and the external forces which support it. Waller has shown how this explains the rarity of open conflict as these structural pressures act to suppress it. The result is a shift to passive resistance.

Children, after all, are usually docile, and they certainly are defenceless against the machinery with which the adult world is able to enforce its decisions; the result of the battle is foreordained. Conflict between students and teachers therefore passes to the second level. All the externals of conflict and of authority having been settled, the matter chiefly at issue is the meaning of those externals. Whatever the rules that the teacher lays down, the tendency of the pupils is to empty them of meaning. By mechanization of conformity, by 'laughing off' the teacher or hating him out of all existence as a person, by taking refuge in self-initiated activities that are always just beyond the teacher's reach, students attempt to neutralize teacher control.[14]

The opportunities for conflict to occur in an active or passive form are determined by the organization of the school. Apathy is difficult where methods involve the pupils in activity. A progressive junior school gives a child little opportunity to close his mind. He is forced to move around, to cooperate with others and initiate activity. Only when more formal methods come into use is there the chance to retire behind glazed eyes while a teacher does most of the work. As the children approach the age of leaving, the extent of this dissociation increases. It is typified by the opening quotation of the Newsom Report: 'A boy who had just left school was asked by his former headmaster what he thought of the new buildings. "It could be all marble, sir," he replied, "but it would still be a bloody school." '[15]

The teacher too can respond to a conflict situation by retreating.

This can involve actual movement. In difficult schools staff turnover is above average, just as the attendance record of the children is below par.

In these slum schools there was only an even chance that a woman who joined the staff later than the beginning of the Christmas term of 1958 would still be there in September 1961; for men the odds were two to one against. Only a third of the women and half the men had been on the staff for more than three years.[16]

Conflict had resulted in the withdrawal of staff to easier areas, although Mays's studies in Liverpool show how loyal many are under unfavourable conditions.[17] Similarly, some teachers become as apathetic as their pupils. There is nothing as tragic as a teacher mechanically retailing irrelevant subject matter to a class which receives nothing. The conflict between them has frozen into apathy. In the secondary modern school studied by Hargreaves, 'for many of the teachers and most of the pupils, life at school was a necessary evil'.[18]

Staff and pupils therefore share common definitions of the conflict situation. There has been an institutionalization, a recognition by both sides that their differences are to be played out according to rules. After an initial jockeying for position, a compromise is reached. Each side gives some ground, but then their relations are regulated. The norms in an organization, in determining conduct, also establish the limits within which conflict is contained. New pupils or teachers have to learn both these aspects before they feel at home in a school. Both will make early mistakes through being too lax or too conscientious. The social structure not only allocates and organizes individuals, it tends to regulate the conflict between them.

This view is not that of Waller who analyses the school in terms of conflict.

The social relationships centring in the school may be analysed in terms of the interacting groups in the school. The two most important groups are the teacher-group and the pupil-group, each of which has its own moral and ethical code and its customary attitudes towards members of the other groups. There is a marked tendency for these groups to turn into conflict groups.[19]

In contrast to Waller, the view taken here is that this division exists, but is often bridged by a shared system of norms. The norms which press on all are usually strong enough to overcome those specific to staff or pupil groups alone, and these act to sustain order. Most schools remain orderly despite the underlying conflict. Booth at the end of the nineteenth century, Lowndes in 1935 and Mays in 1962, all concerned with urban children, pay tribute to this order in schools.[20] The conflict exists, but within norms which usually contain it.

The younger the children, the stronger will be the links between them and the staff. In the infant school and lower junior forms, children tend to accept the values of the teachers. This facilitates the use of methods allowing the children to be active and this in turn reinforces their involvement in work and their cooperation with the teacher. An analysis of secondary schools would frequently reveal staff and pupils as conflict groups. A similar exercise in primary schools would uncover more consensus. But all schools manifest some conflict because they are necessarily restrictive, and all have areas of agreement.

This conflict model does not, therefore, contradict the structural-functional model used in previous chapters. The culture of a school still gives its participants meanings which enable them to work and play together. It is still structured to ensure that roles mesh together into a network through normative pressures. Even the nature and extent of conflict and the resulting punishments are predictable. This conflict focus shows how backstage is related to onstage, how subcultures persist, how friction can be ever present but not destructive. Staff and pupils not only know the cues and symbols that refer to school life on the surface, but also those that give meaning to the clashes between them. The very existence of schools and their organization create conflicts, but the mechanisms outlined earlier guarantee that even in the worst school, some sort of order, however perilous, usually prevails.

With this perspective, teaching is an accommodation to undesirable but inevitable conflicts. Every teacher learns those parts of school life which are going to lead to disagreement. Usually he reaches a compromise, jollying the class along, threatening in a pleasant way, keeping the emotional level down until the crisis passes. In simple societies, difficult personal relationships are avoided or eased by being hedged around with taboos. The uneasy relation between husband and mother-in-law for example is frequently eased in simple societies by the two ritualistically avoiding meeting each other. Similarly teachers avoid getting involved with disorderly groups in situations outside the school, where their authority can be disputed. If action has to be taken in badly defined situations, teachers are cautious, so that if they have to give way, they do not lose face. This avoids the danger of open defiance and enables life to continue fairly smoothly. It is a delicately balanced game between sides that have unconsciously developed a set of rules.

Once conflict is recognized as a part of school life, as in all organizations, it can be faced and used. Dahrendorf[21] has expressed his opinion of this recognition :

. . . First, I should not hesitate, on the level of value judgements, to express a strong preference for the concept of societies that recognize conflict as an essential feature of their structure and process. Secondly, and quite apart from value judgements, a strong case can be made for group conflict having consequences which, if not 'functional', are utterly necessary for the social process. The case rests on the distinction between the two faces of society – a distinction which underlies our discussions throughout this study. It is perhaps the ultimate proof of the necessity of distinguishing the two faces that conflict itself, the crucial category in terms of the coercion model, has two faces, i.e. that of contributing to the integration of social 'systems' and that of making for change.

While hostility between groups is unfortunate, it may serve a useful purpose for the school as a social organization. The rebel, whether staff or pupil, rejecting means and ends and striving to change both, is a dynamic element. Through him, the tendency of organizations to resist change may be overcome. He may be the means whereby new and better relations can result. This is the central argument of J. S. Mill's *Essay on Liberty* and is the reason for tolerating extreme views.[22] The definition of the situation, the feeling of comfort in organizations in which every part of the routine is known, builds up an interest in keeping things the same. The rebel's views may contain truth and his efforts may convince others. Staff, in coming across a new wave of trouble, may be forced to acknowledge that the old ways are not working well. This frequently happens when a school grows larger. Staff begin to fret because heads of departments intervene between them and the headteacher. The larger junior school acquires a Physical Education specialist who changes old practices, tea is made in the school kitchen instead of the staffroom. All feel that things are getting worse. Until this conflict comes into the open new means of organization and communication will not appear fast enough to avoid stress.

Group conflict is even more important in promoting innovations. Every staffroom needs its ginger group, supporting new educational ideas, if stagnation is to be avoided. A passive 'C' stream will receive the same treatment as its ancestors. A rebellious 'C' stream may force some break in the continuity. Schools tend to resist outside interference in their affairs and the teacher within his classroom can shut out pressure for change. The result is often a resistance to new ideas. Conflict may therefore be even more important in schools than in organizations which are forced continually to adapt, through the need to make profits, the influence of research departments within them or the cosmopolitan nature of their employees. Teachers are rarely involved in courses or research which could serve to import new ideas, and the internal organization of the school inhibits their generation and spread. Conflict within the staff, or between them and the pupils, indicates and encourages the need for new approaches.

Conflict can also act as a safety valve, clearing the air. A school can writhe with discontent, until this flares up into conflict, when peace is restored. A complaint from the girls in a junior school that boys playing football were stopping them playing at all, led to football being forbidden in the main playground. The headteacher allocated a small area for the boys and, to stop any discontent, gave them a new plastic ball to play with. This led to a rowdy mob trying only to burst the ball. Its remains were hung on the school railings. This ended the affair, with football carrying on peacefully in the confined space using a tennis ball, without any more hostility.

Conflict also consolidates groups. A staffroom in a tough school generates friendship and mutual support in face of the trials of teaching. This is particularly strong when there has been criticism from outside about the conduct of the school. Similarly a class faced with a harsh teacher will close its ranks, never split on each other, take punishments as a group and support those singled out for attack. A new teacher and his class will adjust to each other through a period of initial friction. Group solidarity contains admirable qualities of loyalty, but may nevertheless be unfortunate as a part of the whole socialization process. The earlier it occurs, the less effect will education have. It seems to build up in the junior school. 'There was a considerably well developed "group loyalty" between the children, to the detriment of staff. The pressures towards conformity were strong, in particular not volunteering information about the frequent cases of bullying and pilfering that occurred.'[23]

With some children such conflicts give rise to the feeling that the teacher is one of 'them' as distinct from 'us'. School is becoming meaningless and there is a steady withdrawal of interest and co-operation. Many writers have pointed to the school situation as a preparation for alienation later on at work.[24] The alienated worker, suspicious of his employer, taking little interest in his job, ignoring pleas for higher productivity, has practised this role as a child to whom school gave little reward and a lot of restraint. In extreme cases attitudes to employers, government, police, anyone in authority are hostile, just as the teacher was one of 'them', to be ignored or opposed.

At the other end of the social scale, schools prepare some to be an *élite*. From an early age they are monitors, prefects and on good terms with the teachers. They grow into this role as leaders and join those in authority, losing contact with the rank and file.[25] The employer, magistrate or civil servant is frequently the product of a public or state grammar school where he was given both prestige and power. The school system tends to mirror divisions in society. As long as these persist in industry, religion, politics, between social classes, generations and nations the schools will be influenced. They can effect change through social mixing, promoting new ideas and stressing objectivity, but they are inevitably conservative rather than radical, because their job is primarily to hand down the culture, not change it.

Competition is frequently used to consolidate or motivate a school. Games are played against other schools, pupils are encouraged to go along to support. The results are read out in assembly. The school is told that it can be proud or must do better. Colours are awarded to the best players and cups and shields displayed in a prominent place. Within the school, forms and houses are consolidated by similar competition. Points are given for matches won, good conduct and academic success, and these decide which is 'top house'. Teachers play off boys against girls or one row against another to achieve good learning and discipline. Even young children in the junior school collect stars and have a points table displayed in the room showing whether 'owls' 'robins' 'finches' or 'sparrows' are winning. 'Lessons can be fun. There is the fun of competition. It is tremendous fun to be able to beat the person who sits next to you.'[26] This quotation from the speaker at the parents' day of a private preparatory school appeared under the newspaper headline 'Fourteen Grammar School Places'. Competition between individuals and groups is an important motivator in school. There is encouragement to see the others as rivals to be beaten in the hurdle race of education. In this, schools again mirror the emphasis on competition which is a feature of our society. Only the infant schools manage without it.

The question is, therefore, not whether there is conflict but where does it exist and how serious is it? A school that is superficially orderly and harmonious will frequently have deep conflicts which persist, whereas an apparently disorderly school may never generaate serious tensions. The worst situation is a refusal to recognize conflict, particularly by the headteacher. Student teachers are particularly prone to suffer in such a school, where trouble occurs behind the closed doors of their classroom, but its existence as a school rather than a personal problem is denied by senior staff. Teachers often claim to be having no trouble from a class that in reality is making their life a misery. This solidarity of staff to sustain their own and each other's authority, which is a fundamental feature of most schools, is made easier where conflict is recognized as a permanent feature. If it is ignored, those members of the staff who run into trouble are denied the support of the rest. They do not like to ask for it as to do so would be an admission of defeat in this most sensitive area.

The chances of staff and children breaking up into small competing groups increase with size. Staff frequently divide over the allocation of resources to departments or forms. All want more equipment, smaller classes and better rooms. Sports, trips, choirs, plays and extra-curricular activities can cause bad feeling as staff try to get children released from lessons. In a primary school it may be necessary to combine forms of different ages. No one wants to teach in the prefab. The married women are accused of not doing their share of extra-curricular activity. These conflicts are solved by the headteacher acting as referee. But if he fails to support his staff against outsiders, another schism will occur. A staff can also divide over personal issues. In one large junior school, staff argued over whether smoking should be allowed in the staffroom. This reached the stage where the smokers withdrew and set up by themselves in the medical room, moving in their own lockers and preparing their own tea. These disputes tend to flare up as the weather gets bad and the end of term approaches.

Similarly groups of children can not only oppose staff, but can dislike each other. A junior school playground can be divided up into territories with defined, recognized and defended boundaries. Stable groups are rare among infants, but from about eight years cliques form, can persist and can oppose one another.[27] At its worst this can develop among adolescents into a protection racket, whereby a physically powerful group dominates and exploits the rest.

Looking at a school from a conflict perspective is important if its working is to be understood. But it would be wrong to finish without stressing that most schools manage to run smoothly even when they are in run-down areas. This description by an American of a junior school in Battersea is a fair example of this.

It is a good school. The children come to it clean and willing, and truancy runs less than three per cent. The classrooms are quiet – quieter than almost any American classroom, because as an ordinary matter nobody – especially not the teacher – is talking. The children are learning what they have to learn with a little over, though their writing will always be better than their reading which does not get quite to the mark. There is nothing nasty about the place : no rowdyism, no deliberate instability, little vandalism, few attempts to interfere with the orderly progress of the school day. The children are not beaten down – indeed, the school atmosphere is much freer than they are used to at home.[28]

This second model of the school raises the problem of how control can be maintained. This is essential if the school as an organization is to achieve its purposes. This is the subject of the chapters that follow. They are based on the assumption that schools are involved in conflicts but that this is itself contained within a framework of values and norms generally strong enough to keep it within bounds and to provide sufficient agreement and order for work to continue.

Summary

In Parts 2 and 3, two contrasting models of the school have been presented. The structural-functional model concentrated on the patterns of behaviour formed by individuals as they performed their roles. It was mainly an analysis of the norms which determined the roles and the processes which ensured that these norms were learnt. The orderly, integrated picture of the school system which emerged was shown to result from a consensus over values and a unified structure of norms.

The conflict model presented in Part 3 focused below the superficial patterns on to the clash of interests between staff and pupils as they interacted. It showed how the same individuals were subjected to contradictory norms and to resulting role conflicts or strains. The school was now seen to be held together, not by consensus over values, but by coercion, the ability of the staff to oppose and contain the interests and actions of the pupils.

These models are not necessarily contradictory. Each deals with different aspects of the same problem of what holds the group together. Using both to examine an organization like a school enables the coexistence of continuity and conflict to be explained. To an observer, staff and pupils seem to have learnt to interact in a routine that is usually orderly and which changes little as some leave and others join. Once the observer looks below the surface, however, tensions and conflicts are noticed alongside the coercion which is used to overcome them. Schools, like all social organizations are held together partly by consensus and partly by force. Both models are needed for an adequate perspective.[29]

Part 4

Schools as organizations

Schools as organizations

6

Order and discipline

The use of two contrasting models for analysis enables the co-existence and order based on consensus and conflict resulting from clash of interests to be detected and reconciled. To do this, the focus will be altered again, to view the school as an organization, fulfilling definite purposes. This chapter is based mainly on the organizational theories of Etzioni.[1] It examines how order is maintained in a school by concentrating on the way pupils are controlled, in the interests of both academic achievement and peaceful conditions. As the inclinations of children often conflict with the objectives of the school, the means of making them comply are vital. Attention will be given to the means of exerting power and the response of people to this.

The usual way of examining discipline in schools is to concentrate on individual children. 'Our materials confirm the conclusion that all researchers into the problem of discipline have reached: the pupil who is habitually disorderly in school and defies standard measures of correction is a child with an unsolved personal problem or problems.'[2] This is the psychological perspective. Here, discipline will be examined as a product of factors in the culture and social structure of the school. Individual problems will occur in every school, but within the context of these social factors. Remedial action usually requires both treatment of the individual and adjustment of the situation.

The two models used so far have given alternative ways of ensuring compliance. The school in which there was perfect socialization, ordering of social relations and agreement over means and ends, would achieve compliance through each child internalizing the norms. The school in which interests clashed sufficiently to make children reject the norms, would rely on coercion to ensure compliance. In Etzioni's terms, schools approximating to these two models would be normative and coercive organizations respectively. Remuneration, his third means of ensuring compliance, is not usually applicable directly in schools. Rewards in school, although they ultimately affect the child's adult status, are essentially symbolic, showing the individual his place in the class or school and building up his commitment. Even the stimulus of working for an examination results from the symbolic importance of passing and the hope of future rewards, rather than a direct reward of money or goods.

Consequently the staff use a mixture of normative and coercive power to keep control. Normative power rests on the manipulation of symbolic rewards. Teachers praise, grant privileges, promote or criticize, restrict liberty and demote. They tell the class to work harder or make less noise, praise it for getting on well though unsupervised. A smile, a raising of a hand, a change in the tone of voice, a question, a sigh, and so on are built into the teacher's repertoire. All these depend on the children being involved in the school, sharing its values, accepting its norms. The teacher must mean something to the class for his gestures to have effect. It is useless using normative power if the school means nothing; for esteem, prestige, honours, marks, praise then mean nothing. Indeed, they are often resented because they mark the child off from his peers. Similarly a teacher can spend all his time providing symbolic sticks and carrots, but the class must value these before they can have an influence.

Good morale in each classroom and the whole school is the first essential of good discipline. If the emotional tone of the classroom is one of warm friendliness, pride in good reputation, and group solidarity, every student means to do well. Even the maladjusted child, where aggressive inclinations are generally beyond his control, tries his best to conform.[3]

This discipline actually builds up its own effectiveness. Involvement means accepting and conforming to the rules. This learning is possible only if these are clearly defined for the pupils and they are sufficiently motivated to learn them. Rewards are given for behaviour in line with the rules, but deviations are punished. Each helps define and motivate. Sending a child to the head to show him good work or be given a house point underlines that this is approved behaviour and encourages its repetition. Making a child write out 'I must not cheat' one hundred times points out the norm and discourages violations. Handing the junior a star or black mark teaches him to value or avoid these. For full effectiveness, each must be accompanied by due ritual or the impact will be lost. The teacher who hands out stars or detentions almost as asides is devaluing the currency on which he depends.

Normative power rests on involving the children in the culture of the school. The enthusiastic junior school child is really hurt if teacher gets cross, the secondary school leaver may see this as funny Studies of disciplinary measures show that most teachers employ this type of control, using their personal esteem and that of the school to get their way. In a British study the most frequently used deterrents were urging on, reprimanding and keeping under constant vigilance.[4] In an American study censure, depriving of privileges and verbal appeals were highest.[5] All these are normative controls.

Normative power is found at its most obvious in the infant school. Children may be guided, pushed, even carried to get them into the right place, but this is rare compared with a manipulation of the child's need to receive prestige and affection, and his dependence on the teacher for this. He is shamed into behaving well by such remarks as 'Oh, John, I thought you were a big boy', 'You're too grown up to behave like that – show me how grown up you can be.' The teacher expresses her disappointment with the child, surprise that such a good child could be so naughty. Control is exercised as it is with young children in the family, by using their need for love and security, and their anxiety lest it may be withdrawn.

Normative power is also used by manipulating the involvement of individual children in a clique. A junior school class will often 'shut up' a persistent talker. A teacher often moves a trouble-maker to where there is no one to support him in his mischief. A class is kept in so that it will exert pressure on those responsible. Etzioni calls this normative-social power, because it relies on grouping among the children. It can, however, be used by rebellious pupils to reduce control, for support from peers can sustain a trouble-maker and a teacher trying to get the class to exert pressure may only make it close its ranks against him. Again, effective normative power depends on the children being involved in the school and the teacher being respected. 'For humans, the most powerful rewards and punishments come from the particular group with which one wants to be identified – that is, whose members one imitates; the group to which one wants to belong.'[6]

Normative power is never sufficient by itself in schools, but in colleges little coercion is necessary. In colleges of education there is a common purpose and interest in teaching. Most are identified with teaching and are learning the professional role. They have absorbed the norms and values which enabled them to succeed at school. They value esteem and prestige given for success as future teachers. In these circumstances normative controls are strong, each feeling constrained to behave as a teacher should behave. Consequently there is a highly developed sense of right and wrong and little need for extensive regulations. In higher education generally, motivation tends to be strong; moreover selection before entry and examinations afterwards eliminate those who are likely to respond in the academic field.

The discussion in Chapter 5, however, has indicated that force is common in schools. In the American study force was only used in about 10 per cent of disciplinary cases, if detention as well as corporal punishment was included. In the British studies, detention and corporal punishment were ranked as the seventh and ninth most common deterrents. Coercion is probably more common. Teachers may be using ridicule and deprivation when they place a child in front of a class, but this is also a coercive action. The child is moved physically, often with threats, often with the teacher looming over him. A noisy procession through a corridor is checked by shouting and pushing. Further, teachers are unwilling to admit using force, but minor slaps and slipperings still occur.

Each of these kinds of power is accompanied by a dominant form of involvement among the pupils. The school in which normative power is exercised tends to involve the children morally and emotionally. This is either an involvement in the values and norms of the school or in the small groups within the school. The pupils conform to the school's idea of right and wrong, satisfy their needs within it and show affection towards it. This involvement enables normative power to be effective and is stimulated by it. Coercive power, however, is accompanied by degrees of alienation. The children reject the values of the school. They can be passive towards it or actively hostile. The degree of alienation tends to increase with the additional use of force. It is at its extreme in approved schools, where a reliance on force inevitably causes alienation. Indeed the dilemma of such institutions is to minimize the use of force to try to win over the boys to the values of the school.

Alienation in schools is not only the result of the use of force. The persistent absence of rewards for some children can result in loss of interest or in actual hostility. In such cases alienation can precede the use of force, which may soon become necessary to counter the trouble caused by groups formed in this way. Alienation can also result from the environment from which the children come. The older residential parts of large cities still contain families that do nothing to support the schools or discipline their children. J. B. Mays's work in Liverpool has filled in the background of statistical studies which show how the unskilled working class failed to benefit from education.[7] Inevitably these sources of alienation combine. Teachers in 'dead patch' areas resort to force because large numbers of children receive no rewards through education and come from environments which make school values irrelevant. The children dissociate themselves from the school which fails to attract them.

Bernstein has suggested another relation between the unmotivated working class child and the tendency for coercion to be common in his relations with teachers.[8] Unable to speak the formal language of the teacher he antagonizes him by using the public language that is all he possesses and which is suitable only for use between equals. The teacher is annoyed at being addressed in terms which he sees as lacking in respect. The situation is aggravated when large classes and poor conditions eliminate any chance of understanding developing through close personal relations, but the lack of a formal language also stops the use of normative controls. These are symbolic, manipulating feelings of shame, responsibility and ambition, and relying on the use of an elaborated code of speech. The working-class child, only possessing a restricted code, cannot comprehend this method of correction. The only means left is to threaten or use corporal punishment. When a teacher says that this is 'the only language some of them understand', he is expressing a rather complex idea in simple terms. But a more wasteful situation could not be devised.

This situation is mirrored in the home. Middle class parents try to interpret their children's motives and reason with them on this basis. They use an elaborated code to remind them of what good boys or girls should be. Punishment too is rarely physical, but more a manipulation of the children's need for affection. They teach their children the language of normative control and prepare them to respond to it in school. Working class parents, often with larger families in poorer homes, a situation parallel to the large class in a poor school, are concerned with the consequences of their children's actions rather than their intentions. 'Don't do that' is more common than 'why are you doing that?'; 'shut up' or 'take that', than an explanation. There is consistency between treatment at home and at school. Remedial action would have to affect both.

Normative and coercive means to ensure compliance are therefore not only put into practice through language, but the balance between them is largely a result of the types of language which the pupils have learnt. Because schools are usually somewhere between heaven and hell, and contain children from a variety of backgrounds, both approaches become necessary. Teachers are inevitably both despots and friends to their pupils for they have to ensure compliance through some combination of the normative and coercive. Further, although pep talks, ticking off, boosting prestige and manipulating small groups may be accepted as fair, ridicule, overdoing black marks, and favouritism are considered unjust and can alienate as much as physical punishment. In contrast, coercion will often be accepted as fair. The implication of this for the teacher's authority in the classroom will be discussed in the next chapter. But the combination of power used will affect the teachers' approach to the job and their satisfactions in it. Personality is important in determining whether a teacher is friendly or hostile, but just as important is the type of compliance in the school. The most benign teacher will harden where force and alienation predominate. 'Flogger' Keate would soon soften in a progressive junior school. Gabriel's research into the emotional problems of teachers has shown that infant and junior teachers express greater pleasure in teaching than do those in secondary modern schools.[9] The most significant factor is the satisfaction of the primary teachers in relation to the personal aspects of school life, appreciation, praise from children and parents and the happiness of the pupils. The teachers studied were involved in expressive activity, satisfying not only the children but themselves. This indicates compliance based on a common acceptance of norms. Teachers in secondary modern schools mentioned negative attitudes to work and authority as the most frequent cause of concern, whereas this was negligible in the primary school. Here there was less opportunity for need satisfaction on both sides. This study, however, was made before secondary modern schools had much time to settle down after the reorganization of secondary education and before the movement to more examination-based work got under way.

This suggests that while all schools ensure compliance by a combination of normative and coercive power, the balance swings as the children grow older. Young children tend to accept the values of school and teacher more readily than the secondary school child. The primary school itself is organized to meet emotional needs by retaining the class teacher and minimizing social distance between him and the child. Work is arranged to allow more freedom in the choice of means and ends. There is a wide variety of activities of short duration. Children under seven rarely establish stable social relations, so reliable support to oppose authority is missing. Finally, the teacher receives support from parents at the primary stage and like them retains the respect and friendship of the child. The secondary school child has more experience on which to base his opposition to authority, and in addition parents and schools may have different objectives, particularly in the secondary modern school where even the interested parents may lose heart at this relegation following the eleven-plus. The individual child can also rely on support from his friends in his opposition to authority. Furthermore the school and his world of leisure are now poles apart and what goes on between nine and four often seems dull beside the glitter of the evening. This progressive dissociation has been summed up as follows:

First and second year boys are often a pleasure to teach, and respond well to the variations in curriculum and method which are possible in view of the lack of any kind of academic pressures. By the time they are third year, however, they become dimly aware of their true positions; educationally speaking they have been sold down the river.[10]

This is aggravated by the selection process. Streaming in the junior school and selection for secondary education have the same result of concentrating the rebel and the retreatist in the same class or school. The lower streams in the primary school and the secondary modern school have the majority of trouble-makers. Selection, however, also occurs between the same types of school. Parents soon detect which school has the best facilities, the best teacher–pupil ratios, the best examination results, particularly at primary level. The interested, mainly middle class parents, get their highly motivated children into these schools, while others receive more than their share of difficult cases. This is a self-fulfilling process, for the school judged as inferior will soon become so, once this selection has had its effect. Private and state grammar schools, selective on social and academic grounds, have the least problems. Schools in the poorest areas have the worst facilities, least parental support, worst teacher–pupil ratios and the most alienation. Coercion in a school is not necessarily a sign of poor teaching, it is a sign of an uneven distribution of problems.

The balance between normative and coercive is also affected by the controls existing in the life of the pupils. Children are subjected to combinations of the two means of control, but in different amounts. The young child is turned into a social being through his dependence, mainly on his mother. She rewards and punishes by giving and withdrawing her affection. But the child is also forced to behave properly. The use of coercion tends to be more prevalent among poor families in poor accommodation, than among the middle class. The latter skilfully manipulate the child's need for affection, playing on his anxiety to produce conformity, and motivation towards achievement. A child of the unskilled working class, tending to come from a large family in inferior accommodation, is subjected to increasing coercion.

Inevitably these differences affect the work of the school. A middle class child will not only be motivated at work, but will also be accustomed to control through a withdrawal of esteem. The goodwill of teachers, or a school position of high prestige, will be valued. The child used to physical force will be less capable of responding to normative control. The school will not offer rewards which attract, nor punishments which deter. Ultimately the school alters the balance in such cases and uses the punishment to which individuals have been accustomed at home. Orderly working in schools (or indeed in any organization) can be achieved only if pupils are responsive to the basic objective. If they are not alienation is inevitable and there is a resort to coercion in the form of corporal punishment, isolation or detention. Exceptional teaching can overcome these limitations. A school can claim the loyalty of very difficult pupils and in consequence, not only use little force, but create a new moral outlook among its pupils. The day school, taking up the smaller part of the pupils' time, is in a poor position to do this and the older the children, the less likely is anything but superficial change possible.

Coercion, however, is preferable to disorder. Further, mild coercion is frequently necessary to overcome resistance to educational objectives. Highfield and Pinsent's survey in 1949 showed that 89 per cent of a cross-section of teachers wanted corporal punishment retained in the last resort and 78 per cent were 'strongly in favour of corporal punishment used with discretion'.[11] The Newsom Report of 1963 found that nearly all heads thought it necessary to retain corporal punishment for boys but that it was rare for girls.[12] The Plowden Committee on primary education, reporting in 1967 found that 'The overwhelming majority (between 80 and

90 per cent) of the teaching profession are against the abolition of corporal punishment, though few support it except as a final sanction'.[13] In the postwar period, attitudes seemed to have changed little. However, this is an advance on the days when 'I never remember seeing my headteacher in school, when he had not a cane hanging by the crook over his left wrist.'[14]

The reason for the persistence of corporal punishment may be in the cultural definition of the teacher's role. After studying the responses of American teachers to the misdemeanours of children, Wickman[15] states that:

Those problems which transgress the teacher's moral sensitiveness and authority or which frustrate their immediate teaching purposes are regarded as relatively more serious than problems which affect for the most part only the welfare of the individual child . . . we would be led in the direction of compliant, submissive, dependent behaviour as more desirable to teachers than aggressive, experimental, independent behaviour.

If teachers want to teach in the sense of organizing, transmitting and acting as models, anything that interferes is to be eliminated as quickly as possible. Under the pressure of the normal school day, punishment is the simplest way of getting the compliance that enables the role to be played.

Discretion is always necessary, however, to avoid alienation. Teachers manipulate children with symbolic rewards and punishment, resorting to force only when these fail. Further, those who are involved in the school will suffer only temporary alienation if they are disciplined into obedience. Firm action, short of physical force, will often check a child sufficiently to remind him that he is running a risk of losing the security of belonging to a community that is satisfying his needs. To send a child out of the room or in front of the class is a severe punishment for many, because it cuts them off from the pleasures of communal activity.

Normative power has three main advantages over coercive. First, the severity of force must be limited. Once used, it is difficult to make it any more deterrent. Once a boy is thrashed he knows he has met the worst corporal punishment available, thus the teacher's room to manœuvre is limited every time physical force is used. Second and more important, force increases the tension between teacher and pupil and may aggravate rather than remove the cause of the trouble. If a class is troublesome the object is always to keep this in check as calmly as possible. Teachers who genuinely lose control and hit out have raised the tension to breaking point. An experienced teacher will always punish without raising general opposition. Frequently he will use a promise to drop coercion as an incentive to better behaviour. But coercion can also lead to withdrawal, lack of initiative. This is a breaking off of interest, because there is no advantage left for the individual to remain involved. Coercion alienates in a school not so much because it violates the freedom of the children, but because it removes satisfactions that children derive from being there. However uninterested a pupil is in timetabled work, school is a place where his friends are. If they are all pushed around too much, even this pleasure is removed. Keeping the tension low is a way of preserving involvement in the school and classroom, however superficial this may be.

The result of alienation, on any scale, is to create dissident, disinterested groups, who will try to soften or undermine the coercion. In school, the circle of events starts early when the unmotivated are first singled out for punishment. Every attempt to stop misbehaviour by penalties increases the alienation and the ties among the group punished. Soon they will have no interest in work and will become a clique supporting each other against the will of the staff. In the worst schools they can set the whole tone, determining the standards of behaviour. While staff may keep the façade of work going, particularly where examinations can be used as a lever, relations among the pupils and between them and the staff are controlled by informal, unofficial leaders. Such leaders are frequently children alienated very early in their education and concentrated in a few schools as a result of the selection process.

The third reason for preferring normative power is that it is continuously effective, not being dependent on the presence of a teacher. A group of unsupervised pupils will rarely lose all control. Schools are like churches, museums and libraries, they have an air of control about them. Just as voices are hushed in church so schools usually inhibit completely uncontrolled behaviour. At the extreme, a strong teacher can practically consecrate his room so that the children almost genuflect on entry and act with humility and reverence throughout the lesson. Conversely other rooms seem to stimulate disorder. But apart from backstage areas behind the gym, in the grounds, around the sheds, in the hidden areas of the playground, the school as a whole contains its pupils, inhibits their behaviour and reduces their rebelliousness. However liberal the régime it must still restrict the child's liberty and at the same time ensure that the consequent frustration does not overflow into excessive aggression. This usually means using coercion.

These three reasons for minimizing the use of force also affect the teacher. Wickman in America and Gabriel in England have both shown that teachers are mainly concerned with obtaining academic results and maintaining their authority. Both are more suitable to symbolic manipulation than the use of force. Children will work or be respectful if they feel normative pressures to do so, but force, however effective onstage, cannot penetrate behind the scenes. Enough work to get by, enough respect to avoid punishment, may be all that is achieved. As teachers need respect, they have to establish a climate in which it is given. The punitive teacher may build this up successfully, but it is his consistency, fairness and drive which matter more than his ability with a ruler on the hand or a slipper across the seat. If force alone is used, alienation will ensure that he will be frustrated.

Rewards and punishments in schools

Teachers use a variety of incentives to motivate their classes. Some of these are material rewards such as allowing the children into the playground or giving a second helping of sweet. But mose use the attachment of the child to the formal or informal life of the school or the teacher. In their *Survey*, Highfield and Pinsent record the order of frequency in which various incentives were used on difficult children and their relative effectiveness. The sample was drawn from children of all ages in all types of school.[16]

The incentives are ranked below according to the number of pupils to whom they were applied:

Boys	Rank order	Girls	Rank order
Appreciation	1	Appreciation	1
Good marks for written work	2	Good marks for written work	2
Interest	3	Public praise	3
Public praise	4	Interest	4
Success in test	5	Success in test	5
Class treat	6	Class treat	6
Good marks for team	7	Good marks for team	7
Made monitor	8	Made monitor	8
Leadership	9	Leadership	9
Good report to parents	10	Good report to parents	10
Material reward	11	Material reward	11

The rank orders for reported effectiveness are:

Boys	Rank order	Girls	Rank order
Congenial work (interest)	1	Congenial work (interest)	1
Quiet appreciation	2	Made monitor	2½
Public praise	3½	Quiet appreciation	2½
Material reward	3½	Public praise	4
Good marks for written work	5	Good marks for written work	5½
Class treat	6	Favourable report to parents	5½
Made monitor	8	Leadership	7
Leadership	8	Class treat	8
Favourable report to parents	8	Material reward	9
Good marks for team	10	Good marks for team	10
Success in test	11	Success in test	11

These lists contain few incentives that are not symbolic rewards. Appreciation, public praise, class treats, good marks for teams, motivate only because the children value the school and class. Good marks for written work, interesting work, success on tests, being made a monitor, good reports to parents, all rely upon identification with the school and the academic ends it serves. Only material rewards lack this normative element. Significantly these are the least used.

This shows how a teacher gets a class to work. He continually stimulates effort and good behaviour by boosting the esteem of pupils in the class, granting them prestige, giving them responsibilities and evidence of success at work. He uses the involvement of individual children in the group by rewarding the class for one pupil's success, thus giving him extra prestige in the eyes of his friends. In learning the culture of schools, children learn to value marks, good reports and public praise. Once learned these symbols are capable of motivating the pupils to play their roles to the benefit of the schools.

This underlines the importance of granting rewards to all as they go through school, but particularly with infants and juniors. Children must experience rewards before they can value them. This is most important when the child is young, because the teacher still satisfies emotional needs, through keeping his work child-centred. Children in infant or lower-junior forms are still wanting attention, still eager to know that the teacher likes them. At this stage they are learning the meaning of the teacher's oral comments and written remarks. If they are not involved, these will mean nothing and will be useless as motivators later on.

The order of frequency of application of deterrents to both boys and girls was:[17]

1. Urged to make effort
2. Reprimanded
3. Under constant vigilance
4. Warned of punishment
5. Deprived of marks or given bad marks
6. Isolated
7. Given detention
8. Deprived of a privilege or treat

After that, the order for boys is:

9. Slight corporal punishment (smack)
10½. Sent to higher authority
10½. More severe corporal punishment (cane)
12. Reported to parents

The order for girls is:

9. Sent to higher authority
10. Slight corporal punishment
11. Reported to parents
12. More severe corporal punishment

Here again, the importance of normative control is obvious. The teachers are relying on the pep talk, ticking off, isolation from friends, close supervision, rather than actual physical punishments or even threats of punishments. The deterrents are symbolic rather than actual, effective because the pupils have learnt the meaning of these actions in home and school. They are least effective where this part of the socialization process has been neglected. In such cases other punishments must be used. The alienation which follows from these merely reinforces the original exclusion from the culture of the school, due to the failure of the early learning process.

However, for this sample of badly behaved children force was more effective than anything else. The cane was more effective than smacking, which in turn had a more lasting effect than detention or warnings of punishment. The cane or strap was available for use for boys in over 40 per cent of secondary modern schools and for third and fourth years of primary schools. It was used sparingly for girls although the majority of difficult girls in primary schools were given slight corporal punishments.[18]

Where children are problems, normative controls may be in-effective. Indeed, they are problems because they have not learned the official norms of the school. Unless there are facilities for in-dividual attention or if necessary treatment, sterner measures usually follow. In large classes the necessary involvement of each child and all it stands for is difficult to achieve. The usual response is to fall back on coercion.

I punish them sometimes, I believe that a child, because he gets angry, understands when an adult gets angry – and for that reason I keep a cane in that drawer. They know I hate to use it, but I will cane a child who deliberately damages other people's property, which means school property too.[19]

This headmaster had built up a good junior school in a shabby area, relying mainly on normative controls such as handing out 'oranges' (compliments) and 'lemons' (complaints). But force was still kept in reserve.

This use of force is a major problem with student-teachers or those early in their teaching career, and looms large among ex-perienced teachers. Lessons can degenerate into a series of promises and threats, slowly losing their impact through repetition until violent action is taken and a temporary lull is gained. As normative controls are the least wearing to apply, the solution is an establishment of an order in which symbolic manipulation is possible. This is often a long job, and requires an effort by the whole school. But the experienced teacher learns to organize classes as soon as he takes them, so that the meanings of his actions are clear. He may use force to underline these. Once this learning has taken place he uses incentives and deterrents, and the class know what he means. In the example quoted earlier, the senior master who could still a school assembly by changing his glasses had made it very clear across the years just what this meant for anyone who went on talking.

In a school, therefore, discipline is mainly established through the use of symbols. It is most efficient if the whole school offers consistent definitions. But beneath these there is coercion if necessary. Waller's view of a school as a despotism is correct because, however well the children have absorbed the school's values, they still comply when their interests are really challenged because they know that they will be forced to and falling into line is more pleasant.

Punishment, from a ticking off to the cane, can serve several different ends. As retribution it is applied because the particular offence deserves a particular punishment. Bullying is often automatically punished severely, because it is morally outrageous. The bully deserves all he gets. The punishments are made to fit the crimes so that any boys found cheating in external examinations are expelled. In these cases, the individual offender is subordinated to the need to punish his offence. Similarly rewards are given because they are deserved and fit the case.

In schools, the individual is often kept in the foreground when considering appropriate action. The aim is to reform him, to stop him doing it again, to encourage repetition of a good deed. Punishment is tailored to fit the offender. The dirty child is made to wash, the slacker is given extra work to make sure he catches up, the persistent offender is sent to the head, who has time to give him a talk and is in touch with outside services if they are needed. Even trivial actions by the best teachers are adjusted to fit particular cases, so that praise is given to those who need it, and those needing correction receive it. Rewards are used to encourage correct behaviour. The efforts of the fidget to stay still are praised. At the first signs of good behaviour from the naughty junior, she is given a house point.

Punishment is also used to deter the offender or others from repeating the crime. Teachers warn of the consequences of going on talking and then punish to stop the chatterbox and show others what will happen if they continue. To make deterrents effective the teacher publicizes the punishment – he makes sure that everyone knows that detention has been given for the offence. There is frequently a ritual fetching of the detention book from the headmaster's study. Boys are sometimes caned for serious offences in front of the whole school. Every effort is made not only to make sure it is not repeated by the same person, but that the rest are left in no doubt about what will happen to them if they copy the action.

All these reasons for giving punishment include elements which help to define the situation. Punishments and rewards underline what is right and wrong. They help drive home the meanings of certain actions. Talking in class is wrong and punishing makes this clear. Hard work is rewarded in public to stress that this is good. This is the crucial function of rewards and punishments in a school as elsewhere. On the surface they may be in the interests of immediately restoring order, but underneath is this vital, latent function of defining what is right and wrong. It is the way the norms are made apparent to all. It is the way morality is established. To an adult, the elaborate and lengthy talk which a junior school teacher gives to the class after it has misbehaved may seem petty and long-winded. But it serves the purposes of increasing the impact of punishment as a way of defining what is wrong and showing them that the teacher is outraged.

The classic advice to new teachers to be very firm at first before loosening up is wise because the initial firmness establishes and defines the situation. Disorder is not going to be allowed and must be clearly defined as intolerable. Each punishment underlines this and explanations for giving it will stress the wrongness of the offending act. This will often mean concentrating on the small disorderly minority. An American study of over four thousand teachers showed that over 60 per cent thought that under 1 per cent of their pupils were trouble-makers.[20] The majority had already absorbed a morality appropriate to school and the symbols which represented it. In primary schools this majority will usually control excessive misbehaviour by the minority. In secondary schools, social support and outside influences may help the pupils resist the teacher and the meanings he is trying to make them accept.

A classroom must firstly have a powerful normative structure. Pupils must feel constrained within a system of order. Secondly, the goals held in front of the children must be within their reach, whether this necessitates only common goals for the class, or goals tailored to individual abilities. The norms define the approved behaviour but, as shown in Chapter 5, there are some who will adopt deviant ways, or give up the struggle, or try to disrupt the whole process if they have no chance of success. If either of these two conditions is not partly satisfied, a state of anomy or normlessness exists and the class or school becomes a rabble held in check only by the use of force. This has been shown to result in alienation from the values of the school, thus aggravating their unreality. Ultimately a class or school depends on establishing an atmosphere in which the children feel involved and constrained. This containment within norms is compatible with individual happiness. The popular teacher is consistent, fair and firm. Children appreciate knowing where they stand. 'Teachers who are strict when you do wrong and friendly when you behave' are liked. Teachers who are 'soppy and let you mess about' gain no respect.[21] In life generally when very rapid change, social disorganization, economic instability or some other factor causes anomy, reactions such as frustration, neurosis, even suicide, become more common. In the 'learning climate' experiments of Lippitt and White,[22] laissez-faire groups in an unstructured situation were neither contented nor hard-working. Visible, attainable goals and clearly defined means for reaching these are conditions which guarantee that the majority will comply willingly.

This applies in all schools for all ages. In the junior school it has been expressed as follows:

Many teachers have found that in working with the entrants class of a junior school, these seven-year-old children are distrustful of new things and do not like many innovations even when they are carried out tentatively and gradually. In the attempt to encourage children to take more responsibility for their work and their behaviour, a teacher has to keep a very careful balance in substituting activity, responsibility and freedom in speech and movement for more formal external control in classroom and school.[23]

Clear goals and procedures not only ensure order, they are a condition of individual satisfaction. Teachers organize their classes to use this convenient overlap.

Such standards can be established best if all those in authority agree over the values and reinforce the same norms. The pupils must be subject to continuous reminders that the school stands for hard work, good behaviour, efficient movement and so on, and continuous reminders that these are appropriate ways of performing the daily round. Once established, this control is rarely apparent, for it will be inside each person involved. If parents can be persuaded to stress the same values the impact will be even greater. In an experiment in a difficult school in the West Riding of Yorkshire, Clegg reported that a tightening up of control in the school, combined with an effort to make parents responsible for the behaviour of their children, slowly created an improvement until a school noted for its delinquency became a model of good order.[24] Significantly staff were 'disciplined' as well, had to sit among pupils at dinner and were stopped from making a quick getaway after four o'clock. This climate of order is the basis of school life, the prerequisite of any progressive experiments. Underneath it is the threat of force, but the stronger the social controls, the less frequently need violence be used.

Many schools are orderly and the pupils not only work well, but are happy in their security, but it is doubtful if many utilize rewards sufficiently. They are usually poorly distributed, lavished on a few while a majority rarely taste them. Yet rewards are as potent a means of control as punishment and do not increase tension. The 'boys', the troublesome minority, are starved of rewards early in their school careers. They obtain satisfaction through their group membership, in opposition to the school which has frequently given them nothing. At a later stage, rewards, if given, are rejected because they are part of a system that is alien. The ultimate aim of

E

rewards and punishments is to build up discipline inside the individual. But punishment alone only alienates, and many never
receive the rewards that would lead to such an acceptance of the
codes stressed by the school. In this sense disorder is the result of
bad teaching. Individual teachers find it difficult to extend their
authority over the whole class because the trouble-makers have
not been involved throughout their educational career. Consequently
force has to be used because the basis of normative order has not
been established.

7

The authority of the teacher

One repetitive theme in this analysis of schools has been that they have influences in the moral and social spheres as well as spreading knowledge. Indeed, it was argued in Chapter 1 that schools not only hand down a blueprint for living, but sort children out so that each learns those parts of the blueprint necessary for the positions he will occupy in adult life. It is because education, as the organized part of the socialization process, has so many faces, and because schooling has been lengthened and emphasized, that teachers need to have real influence. For a teacher to exert this, not only academically, but morally and socially, he must not only be able to establish control, attention and motivation, but this power must be voluntarily accepted by the children. They must accept that it is legitimate for the teacher to exercise power. The teacher must have authority, the right to be obeyed, not just have the means for getting his commands accepted.

The difference between power and authority is crucial. In the last chapter the means of power were examined. But power, the ability to get obedience, can be a barrier in education unless it is accepted voluntarily. Alienation and all it implies in lack of initiative and effort, in the rejection of all that the school stands for, results from excessive pushing around, whether physical or verbal. Education is impossible if obedience has to be imposed. Only when children grant the teachers the right to exercise power can they exert their full academic and moral influence.

The distinction between power and authority is most important in determining those factors which lead pupils from merely yielding to power to seeing its use as justified. A teacher in a school is in a position where he has to lead. Similarly the pupil is surrounded by constraints defining his position as subordinate. Each is in a situation where the distribution of power has been decided outside their control. This distribution is backed by all the external forces of the education system and is sanctioned by law and morality. Waller describes the position as follows: 'A social situation has been set up and its pattern has been determined The pattern is one that calls for a leader. The pattern governs also what the leader shall do with the led. This is institutional leadership.'[1]

However, while there is no doubt that teachers are obeyed mainly because of the position they occupy, this may not lead to obedience being freely given. Pupils may grant a teacher authority because he has the status of teacher and because this gives him the symbols, means and supports of power. But in a time of rapid social change particularly, all the bases from which authority can be derived are also changing. In the remainder of this chapter, the effects of these changes will be examined. While the source of the teacher's power and influence remains institutional, it will be argued that the basis of authority has been changing. In the junior school this change has been going on throughout the century. In secondary schools it has been more recent and probably less understood.

For the individual teacher, the school gives a choice, from which means of exercising power can be selected. The teacher has a positional status in which rights and responsibilities are determined by the social structure. There are rewards and punishments to employ, procedures which are backed by those above, customs hallowed by time. In addition each has a personal status. A teacher brings professional training and experience from previous schools, and combines these with the ideas and procedures existing in the new school. The final blend must be acceptable to other staff, as well as to the pupils. Establishing the right to be listened to and respected, getting authority accepted as legitimate, is the basis from which teaching starts.

In the last chapter, normative power was seen as preferable because it could lead to children internalizing school values. Once this has happened, motives for learning and obeying are no longer ulterior but internal. The behaviour demanded usually seems reasonable and natural. But once teachers are granted authority, they are given respect and attention as a consequence, and not only because they are giving instructions backed by power. Indeed, specific means of control can become superfluous, for teachers can depend on their authority in all circumstances, whether the children welcome the action or not. Their right to respect becomes a norm, binding those involved. Fortunately most teachers gain this position at some time in their career. Suddenly they feel on top of the job, however difficult, and the confidence extends their powers as educators as well as disciplinarians.

Max Weber formulated three grounds on which authority could become legitimate.[2] The first was rational-legal, obedience being granted to rules, procedures, laid down independent of any particular individual. This is Waller's institutional authority. To Weber it was associated with the growth of bureaucracy. In schools it applies to the procedures which have been established. A teacher's authority is partly derived from the laws which relate to education generally, or to that in a particular school. He marks the register, and reports absentees; this is accepted as legitimate because he is a neutral agent in a legal procedure which binds him as well as the class. If the headteacher insists on all classrooms being vacated during break, and this is written into school rules, the right of an individual teacher to clear rooms is derived from these regulations. The authority granted to those in command by virtue of the rules they are enforcing depends on the acceptance of the rules as reasonable by the people at the receiving end. The class obeys the teacher with less complaint when it sees that his actions are derived from regulations for which he serves as agent. This type of authority is common in complex modern societies run on bureaucratic lines. Teachers frequently have to enforce regulations which they neither make nor interpret.

Traditional authority, Weber's second type, rests on loyalty to long-established ways of doing things. These become sacred, vested, inviolate. The leader represents this establishment and the followers learn to value the social order. Authority is seen as natural because things have always been arranged this way. The older the school, the more likely are the cultural traditions described in Chapter 2 to remain as a force. If they do, teachers can be secure because their authority is not questioned. But they are bound within the traditions in the same way as the pupils, and their freedom to change the curriculum or social activities is restricted.

Both rational–legal and traditional authority are impersonal, normative, institutional, derived from laws and customs. In direct contrast is authority legitimated by the influence of the leader. This is based on charisma, personal magic, typified by the prophet and his disciples, the hero and his warriors, the dictator and his followers. Some teachers exercise extraordinary powers over children by projecting their personalities, a state of affairs based on emotion rather than reason. All try to consolidate their authority by exhibiting qualities of learning, humour, athleticism, energy, dignity and so on, which may result in children seeing the power they wield as legitimate. Soon this recognition becomes a part of the norms of the class and authority is sustained without the need for the permanent exercise of the charisma.

Weber's analysis has been criticized for being too arbitrary in its divisions. Most teachers can rely on some combination of all three. Most important has been Parsons's addition of professional authority based on the possession of skills.[3] This is not just a consequence of being part of a bureaucracy obeying laws and procedures, but relies on the confidence of the client in the professional's competence. It has already been argued that teachers lack many of the attributes of professionals such as doctors or lawyers, but they still have the crucial asset of a body of knowledge and skill, so far in excess of the pupils that they have to be taken on trust. Pupils generally accept what the teacher says as the truth. They are rarely in a position to challenge his knowledge and have to take most of what is said on trust. In the moral and social fields, however, older children particularly may challenge the teacher's authority.

These four ways of obtaining willing obedience to commands, can be gained through many types of teaching situation. Charisma is a relation between the individual children and the teacher which is emotionally loaded. But the teacher often emerges as most magnetic when addressing a whole class or school. It can be the sum of many individual relationships or the product of a group reaction. Similarly, teachers can establish a claim to be obeyed, because they represent laws or traditions, through their contacts with both individuals and groups. Their professional skill too can be utilized in a variety of situations. However, a large school, sticking to a specialized, subject-centred, formal curriculum, will make any profound influence by any one teacher unlikely. On the other hand, a progressive, child-centred junior school will not have the procedures or traditions that can serve as a base for authority. Both may be giving a first-rate education.

The social structure of particular schools further determines the opportunities for individual authority to be made legitimate in a particular way. Infant and junior schools, where a class is mainly taken by one teacher, offer more opportunities for exercising charisma, and at this age children are more susceptible to adult influence. This also enables staff to introduce 'traditions' overnight. Consequently, the authority of primary school teachers tends to be firmly based. Established secondary schools, particularly if they have boarders, tend to have older traditions on which the authority of staff and prefects can rest secure. Further, these are often selective schools, giving more scope for the exercise of subject knowledge as a means to authority. In others, efficient regulation pervades the school and authority is supported by neutral, effective school rules. Unselective secondary schools have the most precarious foundations for authority.

With very young children, school organization can be extremely fluid. Infant schools allow considerable freedom for children to work outside the classroom. In the new 'open plan' school buildings, there is no classroom in the traditional sense. Here teachers have dispensed with many of the institutional props of their authority. But there is a steady movement back to formal organization as children get older. Outside the infant school, most teachers have to establish their authority in a classroom, formally laid out, in which they are at the focus of activity.

In the majority of schools, pupils have absorbed sufficient of the traditional and contemporary norms to make them accept the authority of teachers. Even with the most difficult children, the most inadequate teacher still manages to retain some element of control. The pupils are at least contained within the classroom, and even the toughest gang will hesitate to stage a walk out. Indeed, even without a teacher in the room, such a class will rarely spill out to create havoc elsewhere. The children feel that rules exist and affect them. Something has been internalized by the most resistant of pupils. Obedience is to the norms rather than to particular teachers, and these generally act in the direction of order. All teachers start with the advantage of being able to reflect accepted conditions; they work with a cultural definition of the school as a place where order is expected. In turn, each school translates these definitions into specific rules.

Within a school, teachers form part of a hierarchy. External pressures in the form of advice from the D.E.S., the inspectorate, the local authority, parents and employers, flow into the school. The headteacher arranges them into a set of regulations which fit into the internal structure and aims of the school. Staff in turn put those regulations into practice. As they do so they act as representatives of higher powers. The majority of children will have been socialized to accept the control these involve. Even the criminal conforms for the major part of his life; he may rob a bank every now and then, but he performs thousands of honest actions in between. Similarly in school, provided there has been no serious mental disturbance or breakdown in the early transition of the unsocial baby into the social child, serious violations of order will be rare. The school system, therefore, cloaks the teacher in authority, although the cover provided varies widely.

Rational-legal and traditional grounds for exercising authority both depend on agreement that established ways of doing things are right. Both depend on norms. Teachers are backed by Education Acts and school regulations. In extreme cases the courts are sympathetic. But more important, public opinion is no longer hostile to schools as it was at the end of the last century.

Children hated their schooldays, left them behind as soon as possible, soon forgot what they had learned, and when they became parents of the next generation (and marriages took place early) in all too many cases could neither contribute culture to their own children in the home nor readily modify the attitude which they had learnt towards their teachers in their own schooldays. For in some parts the teachers of these times would hardly dare to go home alone, as one teacher whimsically expressed it, to 'the pelting tendencies and rough humour of the neighbour-hood'.[4]

A recent study of five hundred parents in County Durham and North London found that a majority were concerned about their children's education, sympathized with the teacher's difficulties and wanted closer contacts with the schools.[5] The active supporters are, however, a minority. Douglas found only one-third who had shown a 'high level of interest' in their children's work and had also visited the school.[6] The Plowden Committee found that half a sample of manual workers and a third of non-manual workers had never been to their children's primary school.[7]

These normative grounds for establishing authority depend on agreement that procedures are right. The appeal is to the system and its norms. They are rational and standardized, so that as each problem arises it can be referred to them for solution. Norms arising from traditions are sometimes irrational, for the situation in which they evolved has passed. Schools contain elements of both these normative bases for establishing authority. But charismatic, per-sonal authority by contrast is based not on norms but on personality, not on ways of doing things, but on the person doing them. Pro-fessional authority is based on the possession of qualifications and skill in performance. Every teacher employs some combination of normative, charismatic and professional elements to get his authority accepted as legitimate. But in the rapidly changing con-ditions of modern society, when established values and means are challenged, teachers are losing the support of some traditions. This is particularly marked in the decline in religious sanctions for the teacher's position. B. Wilson,[8] analysing the teacher's role says that

Children are exposed to television and other mass media for almost as much of their time as they are in school and generally the values which the mass media present are not those of the teacher. Frequently, too, these alternative values are presented through agencies which confer specially significant weight – highly technical media presenting a readily acceptable, largely escapist, type of material, and providing the fantasy of vicarious success by quick methods, rather than by slow hard work. The message of the media is presented by young people, and is frequently presented in terms of the values of youth against those of age – and the teacher is clearly represented as the voice of the past. This circumstance creates conflict in the teacher's role, but it is a conflict which passes beyond it into the very structure of contemporary society.

As parents have moved towards supporting the school, other influences have grown, undermining both as sources of traditional wisdom.

Tendencies in modern educational practice encourage this challenge to the old order and simultaneously reduce the authority of the teacher as a source of knowledge, or as a person putting into practice procedures, traditions and regulations established in the school as an institution. The emphasis on finding out, questioning, inquiring, encourages children to reject the past as a guide to the present or future. Further it means that children are encouraged to consult other 'experts' outside the school who may contradict the teacher. Consequently the teacher's right to obedience is losing an imporant basis. The increased rate of change also undermines the professional authority of the teacher, because his skills and knowledge may appear irrelevant in the modern world. This affects some subjects more than others. It is most marked in religious education, where increased scepticism withdraws external support from the teacher. Wilson sees this as an historical trend.[9]

Whereas the literati could invoke authority and exert authority, and could ultimately discipline to the point of death those who failed to accept their wisdom, the teacher must cultivate some spirit of heresy within certain bounds in those to whom some more-or-less established information must nonetheless be transmitted. Their own authority must always be tempered and restricted if the right critical spirit is to be drawn forth in the pupils.

The effectiveness of professional skills is reduced by the way they have to be employed. Unlike the doctor or lawyer a teacher must exercise his skill in a formroom, and children can acknowledge his academic ability while creating havoc in his lessons. No other profession has to exercise its particular skills with large groups, many of whom may be unwilling clients. The nearest a teacher gets to exercising purely professional authority is in a class where activity is tightly channelled towards success. This instrumental single-mindedness is rare, however, and the more a teacher has to deal with unwilling pupils, the more useless academic knowledge alone becomes.

The teacher may obtain the voluntary obedience of children through being the agent of a school with strong controls over individual behaviour. But he will have little influence over these. If they are weak he will find it difficult to reinforce them, if they are strong he will find it hard to overcome the children's inhibitions. But he will want to create his own image in the classroom, to stress his authority in its own right rather than as a reflection. Indeed, reliance only on the controls available because of his position as a teacher would be disastrous. Constant appeals to a class to obey rules, sending them to the headteacher, excessive use of stars and house points, slowly reduce the teacher's authority and the effectiveness of these actions. The headteacher in turn loses confidence in the teacher and reduces his support. There is then no alternative but to confine troubles within the classroom. But this means relying more and more on personal authority, the absence of which was probably the reason why over-reliance on the headteacher and the rules occurred in the first instance.

Thus there can rarely be complete reliance on professional skills. However knowledgeable the teacher, some children will be unmotivated; however skilled in classroom control, some will actively or passively oppose. Thus traditional, professional and institutional bases for legitimation have serious limitations, many of which have increased rapidly.

In those schools where authority is most liable to be challanged, the children are least likely to give the teachers respect because of their position. In Chapter 6 this was discussed as a problem of communication due to language deficiencies.

In contrast to the middle class child, who is brought up to respond to the distinction between an office and its content, the working class child confounds the two, so that if there is no personal relationship with the teacher, his function and the subjects connected with it are together disvalued.[10]

Thus Bernstein has expressed the tendency for all but personal authority to lose its effectiveness.

Wilson, too, stresses that personal relations between teacher and working class pupil are the basis of professional skill.[11]

If the teacher is to act as a socializing agent, and to remedy the omissions of the home, he must be in a position to foster a sustained relationship with the child. He must occupy a place in the child's scheme of things, which makes the transmission of values, standards and attitudes of mind one which can occur easily and naturally. Such relationships cannot be prescribed by any blueprint of institutional organization : they cannot be written into a contract. They must occur in a favourable climate where the teacher can cultivate children in this way. This particular facet of the teacher's role is frequently neglected, although its consequences – the sensitive imagination, the appreciation of scholarly values, and the well-rounded, sensible good citizen are demanded perhaps more vociferously than ever before.

Increasingly then the foundations of successful teaching are initially personal and charismatic, as education for all is extended. A teacher can go through the motions mechanically and derive authority from the system of which he is a part. He would be adequate in a well-ordered school, but ineffective when the going was tough. To make a real impact he has to rely on his personal qualities, using them to obtain affection, even devotion from the class, and to gain their respect and submission. At first, this is pre-carious, because it depends on the personal magic not wearing off. The teacher has to be continually exercising it. In time, however, the charisma is accepted and becomes a tradition, part of the defini-tion of the situation. Weber called this inevitable change into traditionalism or bureaucracy, the 'routinization of charisma'. The personal magic gets built into the norms of the classroom.

Charisma operates through satisfying emotional needs among followers. The Red Guards before Mao, the Blackshirts before Hitler and the susceptible at a revivalist meeting are responding to personal magnetism, but are also obtaining satisfaction or release themselves. When the teacher builds up his image and imposes it upon the children he is teaching them to rely on him. The younger the child, the easier this is, but even adolescents feel the need for affection, security and stability. Provided the image matches the age and sex of the audience, they can value it. The infant teacher can act as a mother-substitute, the university lecturer may never meet his students individually, but both can exercise charisma.

Many famous teachers have exercised these personal qualities, and all the great religious teachers had this power over men. Dr Arnold at Rugby, while a distant figure to the boys, was a potent influence in their lives. M. Burn says of Mr Lyward that 'He did possess the gift of power, in the sense that many people trusted him and were willing to put themselves in his hands.'[12] This personal power tends to rub off on to colleagues who gain reflected influence through it. But charismatic leadership, if used to start a movement or inspire a unique type of school, is unstable because it depends on the personality of the founder. When he dies or retires, his words and actions tend to become holy writ. Again, the original magic becomes part of a routine. Arnold's concept of the school, initially radical, became a tradition, increasingly conservative. Progressive education, having won the battle to free the young child from subject-centred methods, is in danger of hardening into principles to be applied. The liberating ideas of Montessori or Froebel become dogma. There are laws of child development, ages when children are ready for reading or writing. Arguments develop over the 'best' methods of learning to read. A dynamic developmental theory becomes a blueprint to follow rather than an inspiration for change.

All teachers, then, need to build up their own image. Some try out many interpretations of the role, noting successes and failures until one that suits them emerges. Failure to experiment in this way may result in an absence of impact, so that they never come across as a person and never carry the class along. Imposing a predetermined interpretation of the teaching role may lead to inflexibility. Primary and unselective secondary schools particularly, contain many children for whom subject knowledge is irrelevant as a basis for authority. These are also the children who are likely to be least influenced by school traditions. Failure to make a personal impact may leave no other ground for getting the voluntary obedience of such pupils.

This search for a combination of personal and positional elements on which to get authority legitimized can be followed in the experience of new teachers arriving at a school. They are in a position to put children under some obligation to them. They may do this not only by rewarding children, but by visibly interpreting rules for their benefit. They soon find out whether the class would like to stay in at break, use ball-point pens, bring pets to school. They can bend school regulations to satisfy these demands. At one extreme of teaching are those who have become completely informal leaders, isolated from the rest of the school, using their own flexible and often officially disapproved methods of assuring their authority with the children. At the other end of the spectrum are those teachers so identified with the school procedures that they almost personify them. Personal magic can be dangerous, just as being a mirror of school rules can be boring. There are teachers who conduct a class like an orchestra. To the observer the lesson is exciting, happy and orderly. The children respond eagerly to every question, every joke, every story. But at the end, it is difficult to think of anything that has been accomplished except a display of virtuosity and fascination. Charisma can be exercised for the vanity of the teacher rather than the benefit of the class.

The teacher can, therefore, actually stop children learning, for this is essentially an individual matter. A child working at a teaching machine is motivated not because the machine has personal authority, but because it is continually rewarding. Indeed, the best work is done when the teacher is forgotten in the pupil's involvement in his task or in self-expression. A. S. Neill has expressed this as follows:

But what is teaching anyway? When I was younger I was more than once called a brilliant teacher . . . even two H.M.I.s said so. I was nothing of the kind. I was doing all the work instead of letting the class do it. I was Billy Grahaming and the poor unsaved boobs were hearkening to my gospel when they should have been telling me about it.[13]

Authority based on the teacher's performance is the prerequisite of good teaching, but it should be as unobtrusive as possible, never an end in itself.

This view of authority as legitimated by personal as well as normative factors is useful because it shows why teachers act in apparently contradictory ways. It has already been suggested that many actions of a teacher are aimed at defining the situation, clarifying the meaning of gestures and actions. When a teacher stops a lesson until 'all the talking has stopped' the class is being reminded that 'when I am talking everyone else must be silent'. The teacher is trying to make a meaning clear. Work is kept as continuous as possible, the day being organized so that there is little idling, thus stressing the norm that school is a place for industry. A pervasive atmosphere is being built up, in which children will learn what is expected of them.

In the settling-in period the teachers need to accentuate their position at the centre of activity. Their first attempts to organize group or individual work in a school where these are uncommon, may end in chaos because these activities remove them from the focus of attention. Slowly they will establish themselves as the agents of forces acting throughout the school. Simultaneously they will build up rapport within the class until they are at the focus, whether visible or not. Then the formal layout of the classroom and chalk-and-talk lessons can be abandoned without trouble starting. The legitimation of authority within the classroom is a priority for good teaching. It is crucial for more progressive methods.

It is doubtful if any teacher arranges his teaching with this in mind. But underneath the haphazard, trial and error methods used by the inexperienced teacher, is a quest for this authority. It means establishing individual relations with some troublesome children. By being helpful, by having a kind word, he is creating bonds to himself. The more the children are exposed to his influence the more effective he can be. The achievement of authority marks the end of the initial period of stress, for the children will now accept instructions without excessive fuss, because they accept the legitimacy of his position.

The qualities involved in charisma are difficult to define. Physique, beauty, charm, strength, humour, voice, mental agility, sincerity, faith may be in the recipe, but the reasons for success are not easily definable, just as personality is not the sum of any set of particular characteristics. What is certain is that some personal impact must be made if the education is to mean more than relaying information and following school routines. Whether it is a calm dignity, or a hectic energy, a strict puritanism or relaxed bonhomie, some impression must be made to qualify for acceptance by the class as a person for whom judgement is voluntarily suspended and to whom obedience is given without hesitation. Different classes tend to respond to different images of the teacher.

Authority then does not depend on any fixed level of formality or force, equality or freedom, nor on any particular teaching methods. Relying on tradition or rules means embodying these. But the tyrant and the timid can both establish their authority by reference to the norms. One may rant about them, another merely hint at them. They can be referred to imperiously or shown to be reasonable in discussion. Similarly the charismatic teacher may be extrovert or introvert, an inspiring chalk-and-talk autocrat or a brilliant organizer of working groups, a dictator or a democrat. With younger children, the qualities may be those which enable them to identify with the teacher as a person. With older pupils, the ability to interest in subject knowledge becomes more important. But no simple definition is possible, for each class with its teacher has unique qualities. This interaction will be dealt with in the next chapter.

The importance of personal factors accounts for the difficulty in teaching people to teach. Techniques, methods of organization and their use in a variety of school cultures can be taught, but charisma is an individual quality. Further, its impact differs with different classes. Indeed the attempts to teach methods may inhibit the development and exercise of charisma by persuading the student to sacrifice individuality to technique. This is complicated by the differences between schools. Each has its own ways of doing things and each has a different normative structure, so that staff and pupils feel that only some ways of acting are right. These norms have to be learned and on a short teaching practice this may be impossible. Obvious features such as how to get supplies of chalk and exercise books, whose blackboard must never be cleaned, which form must never be left alone, which is the way to give out milk, can be quickly learnt, but some are more subtle. Only after a long time in a school is it learned that one form is always allowed to read by itself on Friday afternoons, that marks are given objectively but then altered to 'fit' the teacher's opinions of the children, that 4C have achieved a compromise whereby they are not worked hard, in exchange for remaining reasonably quiet.

A third factor is the difficulty of taking over from a teacher whose authority is based on personal qualities. The understudy replaces the star in the eyes of the audience. The problem can be one of discipline where the permanent teacher restrains the class through the exercise of charisma. But more likely is the difficulty in getting much response from a class that is used to particularly dynamic or inspiring leadership or has been cowed by a dominating teacher. Without this the class remains passive and the student has little time to make an impression for himself. Further, it is just this sort of dynamism that is very personal and therefore impossible to copy.

The emphasis given to personal, charismatic authority in this chapter reverses the usual emphasis.[14] Three related sets of factors seem to justify this. First, the educational turmoil of the period has altered the layout, methods and content of school work on which much institutional authority rested. Secondly, a long and ambitious education has been extended to all social classes. Third, these changes have been part of broader cultural changes which have led to an increasing challenge to the authority of office. Authority in the classroom must come to be established as part of a routine. Its foundations are liable to be increasingly personal.

8

Classroom climate, activity and style of teaching

In all organizations, there are informal groups which form to satisfy each individual's need for security and friendship. The norms of these groups not only tend to run counter to official policy, but are more powerful because obedience to them is the price of inclusion. A school class, whether taught by a class teacher, or a number of subject teachers, develops its own informal structure and norms as well as containing small cliques with their own subcultures. As a child becomes a member of these groups he learns to play his part within them, he learns the norms which define his role. When a teacher first meets an established class there are already leaders and led, sages and fools, comics and butts, and each of these will respond differently. It has become 'our class', valued and satisfying. There are already norms governing work, play and relations with teachers. There are ways of enforcing these norms through the withdrawal or giving of friendship or prestige, threats, even violence, within the informal groups.

A class waiting for a teacher will talk freely, wander about, but some steps are taken to prepare for the next lesson. When the teacher enters, the talking dies down and they stand up. Those who are new or uncertain copy the others, those who don't like the teacher or the school stand up last, but still feel forced to do so, especially when they are the only ones left sitting. Books, pens and pencils are collected together and the lesson starts. Even if this is the first time the teacher has taken them, they still know most of what will happen. One lesson is like any other, provided they follow the routine, things will go fairly smoothly. They see the teacher as one in a tradition of teaching, performing in ways which have changed little and of which they have a clear image. Class and teacher, therefore, behave in predictable ways, slowly accommodating to each other. In a short time the relations between them have become structured, and each can predict the other's moves and actions.

Each pupil will not only respond to the teacher as a symbol, but will see him as a person, feel attracted, repelled or unmoved. The class will get used to his ways, anticipate smiles and anger. The response to demands will now be determined by these personal qualities and the interest built up in the work being done. But there will not be just a series of thirty or forty separate responses resulting from individual needs or interests. The class as a whole develops a relationship as the situation becomes defined and governed by its own norms. Just as each team, a regiment, or platoon, or a club, develop a common response to outside influences, so a school class will give or withhold allegiance to a particular teacher. Most teachers have experienced the feeling that they don't get on with a particular class, while they feel at home with others, although other teachers have the opposite experience with the same classes. This results from the existence of a normative structure of which the teacher is very often not even aware, even though it governs his relations with the class.

Style of teaching

The structure of the relations between teacher and pupils provides the setting in which authority is established. As children move through the primary school, they adjust to each new class teacher. In the secondary school they accommodate to several different class organizations in successive lessons. Further, each class with its teacher varies its relations according to the time of day and year. In the studies directed by H. H. Anderson,[1] teachers became more dominating as each day and term drew towards its close.

Apart from these variations, teachers find it easiest to fit into established routines. These are reinforced by the timetable, apparatus, use of physical space and the proximity of other classes, but are also related to the social structure of the school class. The children are organized on the basis of a routine, and changes necessitate new values, new norms, new statuses and roles. Children may welcome change, but there will be initial confusion as new roles are learnt. If the school as a whole is organized for a particular routine, any teacher and class will be under pressure to conform, and attempts at change will be even more liable to lead to disorder unless the experiment can be insulated. This is easier in primary schools or in remedial classes in secondary schools, as class teaching facilitates insulation.

The commonest division in teaching styles is between democratic and authoritarian, the former trying to establish two-way communication in the classroom to involve the children, the latter teaching without consultation. Most of the experimental work that has been done has been inconclusive, mainly because the definition of these two styles has not taken full account of the complexity of the classroom situation. However, the research has been very influential and provides evidence on the forces which actually define the situation.

The most influential experiment has been that of Lippitt and White.[2] Children aged ten and eleven years from two school classes volunteered to make masks after school. They were divided into matched groups. A pilot study established that it was possible to build up a democratic and authoritarian situation in this task. Adult leaders were then trained in performing as authoritarians or democrats, or in a laissez-faire style. The authoritarian gave orders and instructions, but gave no chance to the group to contribute. The democratic leader, while guiding the group, involved them in decision-making. The laissez-faire leader left the group to produce masks as best it could without giving orders or guiding discussion. The behaviour of each group and the interaction between the individuals within them was noted by observers and evaluated for attitudes and performance. The laissez-faire group performed worst in every way. The democratic group had the least hostility towards its leader and between its members, and performed best of all the groups when the leader was absent. The authoritarian group was more aggressive towards its leader and towards other groups, although relations between the children were as friendly as within the democratic group. The authoritarian group was slightly more productive than the democratic, although the latter worked better when its leader was out of the room. Both were more productive than the laissez-faire group. The conclusions drawn from these results have usually stressed the superiority of democratic methods of teaching, because the children involved are both productive and happy.

The one result of the Lippitt and White experiments which has been confirmed by other studies, is that children neither like the teacher, nor work hard, nor behave well if there is a lack of leadership. Whether democratic or authoritarian the teacher must establish himself as the centre of a system of order. Fleming has expressed this as follows:

The democratic approach has more in common with a dictatorial approach than has often been supposed. It is not laissez-faire. It does not represent abdication on the part of the teacher nor is it an advocacy of self-expression, a complete freedom for pupils without regard to the requirements of others and without recognition of the necessity for technical advice from adults.[3]

The claims for the superiority of democratic classroom situations have been challenged on theoretical grounds. Indeed, if a class builds up its own social structure, any experimental group may be too artificial to allow generalization to real situations. Brookover[4] has pointed to the need to distinguish personal relations in the classroom from the work done. Noting that the authoritarian group in the Lippitt and White experiments managed to make more masks, he examined different styles of teaching in actual classes. High school pupils of sixty-six history teachers were asked about social relations in the classroom and also tested on how much history they had learnt. Brookover's conclusions were that 'apparently students liked friendly teachers better but learn more when taught by teachers who are perceived as less congenial and friendly'. This suggests that there may be a choice between efficient learning, particularly of facts, and happiness in the classroom. It is probably safer to recognize the complexity of the factors at work which limit the usefulness of generalizing. An infant teacher is more concerned with creating a climate of friendship and confidence than a secondary school teacher preparing a class for an examination. Some subjects require a factual basis, others need more spontaneity and creativity. Goals can be short term and mundane, or a vision of adult qualities that the teacher wishes to inculcate in children. Classes differ in the strengths of the groups which support or oppose school policy, as well as the individual capacities of their pupils. Above all, class and teachers are linked in interaction which is governed by norms and what works in one may fail in another.

In American elementary schools, H. H. Anderson and others have shown how different types of teaching produce different behaviour patterns among the class.[5] Observers of actual lessons noted that teachers who tried to dominate a class without taking its wishes into account frequently failed to do so, but the children in turn tried to boss each other. Teachers who were always trying to produce friendly relations, trying to involve the class and consider its views, got more cooperation and the children cooperated among themselves. This tended to confirm the superiority of democratic classroom situations for good staff–pupil relations, although the amount of work done was not measured. Regardless of the meaning of the results, this shows, as do all the experiments mentioned, that a teacher can influence the behaviour of his class. This, however, must be done through the class as a social group.

A skilful teacher is able to some extent to influence the roles that individuals play within the groups and to provide some measure of success for most children. Meantime the class takes on a personality with its own history, its own jokes, its own favourite words, all in some sense a protection from the mass of the school.[6]

This quotation from the Plowden Report on primary education, shows the difficulty of assessing the efficiency of different methods, unless the 'personality' of the class is taken into account.

The tendency for classes to develop behaviour patterns in response to styles of teaching, is one way in which the classroom situation gets defined and values established. The teacher controls many of the factors which define the situation but others emerge beyond his control. In a study of two parallel groups working at the Harvard School of Business, Orth has shown how each developed its own very different working habits, relations with tutors and internal relations.[7] Each had its own way of influencing the amount of work it was supposed to do. Each supported its weaker members in its own fashion. Each had developed its own learning climate. The teacher in the classroom is faced with a group which has its own way of constraining its members. The 'swot' is subjected to enough pressure to bring him into line, for he is ostracized, outlawed, excluded from the class, which demands acceptance of its codes in exchange for bringing friendship and security. The success of authoritarian or democratic methods for producing good social relations or working efficiency depends on this climate. The teacher can influence it, but not by applying a predetermined formula once the class has had time to become a group. The informal structure can affect the quality and quantity of work, the type of behaviour, relations with teacher and all the action which makes up the school day. Above all it will change with different teachers because the class adjusts to each of them in a different way. A class will have its own norms for work and play, but one teacher may find it easy to work with, while another cannot get it to cooperate.

It is also within this climate that authority is exercised. The acceptance by the class of the influence, knowledge and power of the teacher depends on this. The democratic teacher may be a failure or a success according to the ease or difficulty with which his authority is established in a particular learning climate. But as this is not wholly within the control of staff, neither are the chances of success of democratic teaching. Similarly autocratic methods may fail or succeed for reasons beyond the control of the teacher. A school can establish so powerful an influence over its pupils that a particular teaching method always succeeds. In many grammar schools a teacher can succeed through authoritarian teaching because the pupils are involved in a strong, pervasive, academic culture. Many primary schools have such an air of child-centred activity that democratic methods are infallible. But usually the teacher has to adjust his methods to fit the often very different climates within each class. Neither method, authoritarian or democratic, is intrinsically superior; either may succeed in favourable conditions, or fail if they go against prevailing norms.

The methods of communication and control chosen by a teacher do not only have to work within established classroom structures. In a study of 800 primary and secondary children, asked to give the characteristics of a good teacher, Taylor found that children judged teachers by their ability to teach, rather than on personal qualities.[8] He suggests that the children felt a need to be taught and that this was culturally determined. Children seem to learn a definition of teaching that is traditional, or authoritarian, rather than democratic. While this may be changing for the primary school teacher, it implies that progressive methods not only have to be adapted to the norms of a particular class but start with the handicap of not being accepted. Children see them as strange and are suspicious of their value. The definition of the school as a place of order, and the teacher as an authoritarian, may be built into our culture.

Types of activity

Teachers adopt methods and arrange communications in the classroom partly to suit their style, and partly because of the nature of the activity. But neither the class nor individual pupils are passive. The former is a social group that is not only subject to the external pressure of the teacher but concerned with its own internal condition. Similarly individual children are balancing their own needs against the demands of the lesson. As the class works towards completing a task, members will be expressing friendly or hostile views, consolidating or disrupting the group. There will always be expressive behaviour alongside the instrumental. Further, this spontaneous activity within the class accompanies the efforts of the teacher to push it on academically while keeping it together socially. This is necessary because individual learning depends on emotional security and this comes through the group. Efficient learning depends on there being no unsatisfied emotional needs blocking the way. The worried child will learn little, the mentally disturbed nothing at all.

The activities in a school are divisible into the three categories defined in Chapter 2 : instrumental, expressive and moral or normative. Instrumental and expressive action is always accompanied by activity discriminating between right and wrong. Teachers are not only trying to educate children to become moral beings, but are continually emphasizing the need for them to act in a way that will integrate the class and school. Similarly the children have their own codes. A classroom is always the centre of a dialogue over conduct. Whether the teacher and the class are in sympathy or conflict over values, these are the subject matter of many exchanges. This is moral action.

When the teacher points out what is right or wrong, he is defining the situation as he thinks fit. This is more prevalent in infant and junior schools, where the children's behaviour is often under close scrutiny. The class is organized to teach children to respect the rights of others. Priority is often given to establishing individual morality and a consensus of belief in the school. As children grow older, this priority gradually shifts to activity which builds up knowledge and skills for the future. This change is reflected in the way a child's performance at work can become the first concern of the teacher. From the infant school to the senior forms in secondary school there is a movement from moral to instrumental activity. The latter tends to take preference over expressive activity as children get older.

In the small groups studied by Bales, instrumental leaders drove the rest towards completing the task in hand, but at the price of increasing hostility from members of the group.[9] This was relieved by expressive leaders who smoothed out personal difficulties and kept the group from breaking up. In a class, or a group within it, similar leaders will arise among the children. Some will be pushing towards the solution of a problem, while others are keeping the peace. But the responsibility lies mainly with the teacher. Not only must the task be accomplished, but the class as a whole must gain satisfaction from the success. The teacher who accepts answers from the brightest only and sets the pace from them will lose the rest of the class. There must always be encouragement and help for the slower children, breaks in the drive for completion to relieve tension. Most lessons include exercises, periods of questions, anecdotes and activities, which draw the class together, enable some to catch up and give opportunities for self-expression. However hard a class is being driven towards an examination there is always time for activity not directly geared to the task. The teacher acts as expressive as well as instrumental leader, because this avoids leaving part of the class behind in the work and keeps individual children happy and enthusiastic.

The importance of expressive activity has led to teachers deliberately getting to know children as persons and treating them and the class as active rather than passive. Children are treated as emotional and social as well as intellectual beings. But emotional and social needs are also recognized through timetabled expressive activities such as music, dancing, physical education and art, where the emphasis has changed from an established, predetermined technique to free expression. The claim to educate the whole child indicates this stress on expressive as well as instrumental activity. It has the same basic function as activity generated spontaneously within the class or initiated by the teacher. Both aim to release human potential through removing individual inhibitions and through creative, collective experience.

This is made more important by the existence of conflict within the class. Some expressive behaviour will be hostile and disruptive. Some children will be tired of being ignored, unmotivated through lack of reward. Consequently the teacher must counteract this by deliberate attention to reducing tension. Laughing, joking, expressing satisfaction, giving help, bestowing prestige are tools used to keep the class together as it is learning. This is another reason why rewards are preferable to punishments. In keeping the tension down, rewards allow the teacher to work a class hard without fear of disorder. Expressive behaviour may appear irrelevant to the main object of the lesson, but it is often crucial for its success.

There are, however, different problems for the teacher in instrumental and expressive teaching situations. The mathematics teacher may see the job as providing tools vital for future use, but the artist may be aiming at releasing and expressing the imagination of the children. The former may express the usefulness of converting fractions into decimals to gain willing cooperation, while the latter relies on involving the children through satisfying their emotional drives. From the child's point of view one is instrumental, or task orientated, while the other is expressive. One is pushing them towards completing a task, the other is encouraging them to cast aside inhibitions. The music, art and dance teachers run the greater risk of immediate, overt disorder as a consequence of this difference, but the more academic subjects are more likely to lose the interest and attention of at least some of the children. Expressive teachers must be more involved with the class, while the instrumental teacher can remain detached. Both involvement and detachment have their dangers.

The balance between instrumental and expressive activity changes as children get older. In the infant school the developmental tradition dominates, and finding out and developing individual capacity take precedence over instruction. Story-telling, art and craft, dance and singing, are common, and the emphasis is expressive. But slowly basic skills have to be learnt and in the junior school formal work is extended. Teachers lay increasing stress on performance and achievement. The supporters of child-centred education do not deny the importance of learning skills for future use. They see this as best accomplished through the children's own activity. The difference lies in whether the emphasis is given to work as a direct preparation for more to come in the future, or whether it is an activity beneficial in itself, through its effects on the child's values.

In the secondary school, specialist subject teaching reduces the opportunities for influencing the child as a person, as contact is made for short periods only. This is a symptom of the greater stress on instrumental activity, for expressive activity needs close contact between teacher and class to build up the confidence which enables it to occur. Art or music teachers in a secondary school often have a difficult time if they stray from formal preparation and practice. The uninhibited expression of adolescents in music and dancing outside the classroom and the school, contrasts with that inside. The G.C.E. and, more recently, the C.S.E. mean that work is determined by a set syllabus for a majority of pupils. Individuals fit into the scheme or dissociate themselves from it. In a similar way preparation for a job becomes important, and practical work is designed to provide the appropriate skills, rather than serve as an expression of practical creativity. While the grammar school is nearest to this model, geared to external examination and vocational opportunities, the non-selective schools have steadily moved towards this from the more flexible, less academic model drawn by the Ministry and by educationists after 1944.[10]

This shift does not eliminate charisma as a basis for legitimating authority, but it means that it is exercised in subject-centred rather than child-centred teaching. The infant teacher can exercise the influence of a parent on the young child. She is trusted and obeyed through her links with the child. The children have few inhibitions and express themselves freely. She can become an expressive leader. The secondary teacher has most opportunity to gain authority through teaching a subject, particularly if this leads to an external examination. Knowledge and enthusiasm, skill in its communications are at a premium. The ideal now is to produce an appreciation of the subject, a class that effervesces in its work. There is more opportunity to exercise professional authority through the subject. The junior school teacher has to maintain a balance between these positions. Skill in personal relations and organizing children to learn for themselves, has to be accompanied by a depth of knowledge capable of stretching the brightest and interesting the dullest. Similarly, there is a balance between expressive and instrumental activity not found in the infant or secondary school.

Whatever the activity, it still takes place within the context of the social structure of the class. This will affect the rates at which a task is performed, and the role played by each child. Some classes mix freely and have few divisions or conflicts, while others are split into warring sects. One class may be impassive, another volatile, one individualistic, while another supports its weaker members. One may revel in doing repetitive exercises, while another excels at problem solving on the board. One may sing lustily in music lessons, while another makes embarrassed groans. One may dance like a dervish, while another shrinks like the violet. Just as authority and communications have to be established and exercised in such a context, so does the organization of activity.

The class also has its own specialists in instrumental and expressive activity. There are those who are always ready to answer difficult questions, give out books and apparatus. Their enthusiasm keeps up the pace of a lesson. There are others who will always be ready to sing out the obvious answers, laugh at weak jokes, express gratitude and help their neighbours. They like school, the teachers and the class. On the negative side there are those who moan or remain withdrawn, or obstruct and deflate. Just as these reject the school and its values, so they are disruptive in any class which tries to cooperate with the teacher. As a class develops a social structure, children within it become specialists in particular types of action. They play these roles in lessons according to the opportunities which the particular activity presents. This determination of activity in the formroom by the norms of the class as a group has been described as follows:

When the class is formed the first cohesive elements are apt to reside in the subgroups which are based on natural friendships and interests among a few children. Gradually, as the individuals perceive and respond to the teacher, to the broader emotional tone, to the goals and the program – there evolves a group spirit, a common feeling of belonging which now pervades the group-as-a-whole. Under such circumstances one can hear increasing reference of the students to themselves as 'we' and 'our class'. Insofar as the group is capable of satisfying the cardinal needs and interests of these children, it assumes an ever greater meaning and importance to each individual. This, in turn enhances the stability and the motivational strength of the group.

With such an increase in 'we-feeling', there develops in time a structure, a way of organizing the group's daily life. There is a division of responsibilities; there are also various roles assumed by the students, in response both to inner needs and to group expectations. A class has its own leaders, its powers behind the throne, its clowns, pets, executioners and peace makers. As such a role might become the individual's major way of getting status in the group, it is quite possible for some students to hold on to it tenaciously (in spite of the teacher's displeasure if it disrupts the class), because his peers expect him to do so.[11]

It is within this social structure that the teacher has to operate. His success will largely depend on the way he adjusts to the unique structure of each class.

The school as an organization

The school will now be viewed as an organization, serving purposes in the whole process of socialization. An organization is a social grouping deliberately established for a certain purpose. Schools are set up to achieve definite ends. In Chapter 1 it was argued that they were established once a society becomes so complex that moral and vocational education of the young cannot be left to the family, but must be done by specialists. In preindustrial societies, priests or elders, wise in the folkways, suffice, but slowly the teacher, a variety of social workers, youth leaders, medical and legal experts emerge to do their share in turning the child into an adult.

Schools exist to help in this transition in all its aspects. In Chapter 1 these were divided into instruction in subject knowledge and techniques, moral and social training, and preparation for social mobility and change. These are elements of culture, and socialization is the process whereby they are learnt by the young. This is the purpose that schools serve, teaching children the blueprint for living in the society they serve. Instrumental, expressive and moral action in schools serves this end.

What goes on in a school is, therefore, a passing on of culture. The content of education covers all cultural aspects. Just as learning the culture brings mental awareness, a way of perceiving ideas and events, so education is cognitive, concerned with knowledge. Culture also includes means of evaluation and consequently education is concerned with the moral or normative, with what is felt to be right or wrong. It is training the young to behave properly and to hold correct beliefs. Finally, just as culture influences ideas of what is pleasant or distasteful, so education is concerned with establishing taste in artistic appreciation and physical activity. The instrumental, moral and expressive action in school serves these cognitive, evaluative and cathectic functions of culture.[1]

These divisions of culture and their presence in education mean that schools inevitably do more than just teach. This is why education so frequently clashes with what is learnt outside school, for the teacher is also moral philosopher, welfare worker, critic and arbiter of taste. He is engaged in socialization with others who may not share his views, and this process covers all aspects of the child's progress to adulthood.

There are continual shifts in the emphasis given to the various strands of culture. Preindustrial societies laid most stress on moral education as an organized procedure. Vocational preparation can be left to chance as the children follow their parents. Industrialization, bringing more complicated jobs and a division between the occupations of parents and children, results in schools taking over vocational preparation. In advanced industrial societies, priority has to be given to building up knowledge and skills to prepare children for their positions in a very complicated technical system. Aesthetic education, social training and moral education, tend to become poor relations.

These educational ends can be met in many ways. Basically they depend on the exposure of the child to teaching. But this can be achieved through teacher or child-centred techniques, precept or example. The ends can be manifest, intended objectives or occur without planning. They can be reinforced by influences from outside the school or hindered by them. Schools are organized so that children receive the concentrated attention of adults who have themselves been trained to be efficient transmitters of knowledge and values.

The cultural goals served by schools determine not only their internal organization, but their external relations. Parent–Teacher Associations can often reinforce academic progress by involving the pupil's family. They can also be used to gain support for the moral and aesthetic values of the school. Similarly local authority, inspectorate, churches, welfare agencies, further education, youth employment and youth services are expected to support the ends of the school. Where there is a conflict of aims, the staff, instead of establishing links, try to insulate themselves and the pupils from the conflicting influence. Pupils will be banned from a youth club with a bad reputation. Grammar school pupils are persuaded to give up friendships with those in secondary modern schools near by. A critical inspector meets a staff solid in passive opposition. Research challenging established practices is rejected as impracticable.

Internally the school allocates its resources according to the stress put on instrumental, expressive and moral elements. This not only concerns appointment of staff, the importance of certain departments, the formation of the timetable, but the norms built up under staff influence. Manchester Grammar School and Summerhill have different aims and different organizations and procedures to meet these. But effective formal organization requires that there must be no frustration by conflicting informal influences generated among the children. The development of organization theory in this century has been largely concerned with these two aspects, formal and informal.

The organizational ends

1. *Instruction in subjects*

To the observer of a school – its timetable, the activities in its classrooms, its books and equipment, and the interests of its staff – instruction in subjects seem dominating. As the children get older, this is increasingly emphasized. This is not just a reduction of the time allocated for expressive activity. There is the steady contraction of time spent on activity not fitting into a particular subject. Social, local and environmental studies, art and craft, general science, crystallize into specialist subjects. The general activity of the infants changes into the concentration on a few subjects in the sixth form of a grammar school. This is not only the most obvious feature, it is also uppermost in the minds of those most involved. Teachers tend to emphasize this aspect of their work. Musgrove and Taylor, examining the teachers' conception of their role, found that most teachers tended to see the job in terms of subject instruction and moral training.[2] Parents held similar views to those of the teachers, although the latter thought that parents saw schools only as places for acquiring subject knowledge. To a child past the infant stage, school is 'subjects'. While obvious, this is only a recent development, for popular education was initially seen as a moral rather than an intellectual instrument. Even a little knowledge was viewed as a danger to the established social order.

Concentration on academic instruction, however, can be self-defeating, by increasing the alienation of working class pupils. This is probably because they do not share the values of schools. Sugarman, in a study of a grammar school, a comprehensive and two secondary modern schools in London, found that in the two last achievement and conduct were related to the values held by the pupils.[3] Sugarman's explanation was that in the grammar school the pupils had already adopted middle class values or that intelligence was the dominating factor, regardless of their origins. In the remaining schools the values held by working class children could affect adversely their achievement and conduct. Middle class children, not experiencing culture conflict, were not handicapped in this way.

2. *Moral training*

Moral education is bracketed with subject instruction in the minds of teachers and parents as the main objective of education. The greatest weight was given to it in infant and junior schools, the least in grammar schools. Historically this has always been important. Moral guidance, however, is no longer given in any intensive, systematic way, although cultural values and norms are the foundations of all the official work of the school. The religious education lesson retains only a precarious hold in schools. It has been reprieved by the Plowden Report on primary education, although the committee was split.[4] It persists in secondary schools, but often as a discussion of controversial ideas and rarely as direct moral instruction. It has moved from a central to a peripheral place, being seen as a matter of example and influence, rather than instruction.

This change has been rapid. The apprenticeship system which provided a true education for many up to the end of the eighteenth century, was a moral as well as a vocational preparation.[5] The master closely supervised the morals of his apprentices, who were considered as potentially wild and immoral. Popular education was allowed to develop only because it was seen as an instrument of moral instruction. In 1861 the Newcastle Committee still reported on schools as instruments of morality and religion.[6] This stress was inevitable, for the movement towards universal education was religious in origins until 1870.

The decline in systematic moral instruction in schools has been partly due to the rising claims of subject instruction as necessary to prepare for an increasingly complicated set of occupations. Equally, however, it is due to the difficulty of maintaining and teaching morality at a time when there is no general agreement on values. Religion can no longer be used as a complete guide since it lacks its former authority. As the world changes faster, that which is seen as proper today is questioned tomorrow. Technical advances accompany increased scepticism. Improved contraception and the sexual revolution are part of the same general movement whereby old practices and values are challenged.

This is often complicated for the school by the lack of support from parents on moral issues and the values stressed in leisure. Teachers have been shown to be concerned about moral training, but the response they get diminishes with the age of the children they take, particularly those from poor environments. Thus it is just those children who seem to need guidance who are least open to it. In none of the other functions of education does the gap between pupils and staff, whether resulting from differences in age, social class origins or cultural background, so reduce the impact of the teacher and the incentive for him to try to exert influence.

Nevertheless, a school is organized to transmit moral values in all its activities. On the games field, loyalty to school, house and team, perseverance in the face of fatigue, being a good sportsman, a good loser, a generous winner, are important. Last man in at the end of a race is clapped for staying the course; each team gives three cheers for the other: the football team claps its opponents as they leave the field. Pain must be ignored or borne, pleasure expressed without excessive demonstration. Behaviour outside and inside the school is directed by the continuous application of a moral code stressing conventional values. British schools have their origins in the Church; they grew up under religious influences, and have always been concerned with virtue and manners as well as knowledge, as many school mottoes testify.

3. *Social training*

Schools have always been agents of social control. Popular education was not only expanded to bring religious belief and moral guidance, but to make sure that as rural life was replaced by the new industrial order the expanding population would remain orderly. The close personal contact which had controlled behaviour in the village was missing from the growing towns. The provision of schools was seen as a way of 'promoting the diffusion of that knowledge among the working classes which tends beyond anything else to promote the security of property and the maintenance of public order'.[7] Their success has been described by Lowndes: 'The contribution which a sound and universal system of public education is perhaps the most potent of its benefits.'[8] It can extend from a stress on manners to the organization and encouragement of service to the country. Today many senior girls and boys become involved in carrying out voluntary work in cooperation with local social services.

Social training remains important. Teachers do not see it as being as vital as moral or subject instruction, but the schools are frequently seen as the means of combating delinquency, bad manners and poor taste. Unfortunately, in those areas where problems exist, schools tend to be physically inadequate and poorly staffed and the opposing pressures outside the schools are strongest. However, the influence of the school can still be important. Clegg, in a study of thirty West Riding schools, found that the quality of the school had a desirable effect in reducing delinquency.[9] In a description of one of these schools, he showed the success of tightening discipline throughout a school. Parents were brought in without hesitation to deal with pilfering, verminous heads, persistent lateness and sex offences among their children. If they were uncooperative they were treated with the same firmness. Staff, too, were stopped from adopting strictly nine-to-four hours. In this way a blackboard jungle was transformed into a model school. Mays in Liverpool was optimistic about the influence of the schools on the behaviour of children in the area.[10] Hargreaves, however, saw the secondary modern school as a factor in promoting delinquency through its treatment of lower stream pupils.[11] Dell, in a study of schools in Belfast, was guarded, finding that 'there is certainly a measurable effect due apparently to school quality, or some relative factor, but this effect seems to be considerably less than that of socio-economic influences'.[12]

Some schools seem to have few problems while others, drawing pupils from a similar background, have many. The organization of the school must be a factor behind these differences. Sociologists have examined the environment for its effect on performance in school, rather than the school's influence on the locality. Consequently there is little evidence on this point that is not contradictory. Some see the schools as doing a good job in the face of strong pressures from poor home backgrounds. Others see them encouraging dissociation from the values for which they stand, through their treatment of the less able.

The perspective of the school as an organization differs from that used so far in concentrating on means to achieve ends. School A in Chapter 2, an infant school, giving priority to teaching good habits, manners and appearance in a very depressed area, was organized with social training in mind. The headmistress was a friendly, enthusiastic woman, distributing flattery to the children at the first signs of improvements in their behaviour. She had appointed two members of staff who seemed to her ideal for this purpose. The reception class was taught in a small but immaculate room. The parents of each new child were shown over the school, had a talk with the headmistress and were repeatedly thanked for their efforts once the children began to dress, look and behave better. The teacher in charge was young, attractive and very smart. She concentrated on getting the children to behave politely to herself and to each other. The other classrooms were extravagantly decorated with the artistic efforts of the children. There was little emphasis on basic skills in reading and writing until the children reached the class of the headmistress just before going on to the juniors. The school day was still mainly an exercise in learning the social graces and stimulating the imagination. Again the two mistresses in charge had been picked for their abilities in this direction. The buildings of the school reflected their efforts. They were clean, freshly painted and bright with pictures. Morning assemblies were an exercise in good manners, giving thanks and singing well-rehearsed hymns. The local parson frequently attended to hear and praise the children's efforts. The school was a 'starting' school in the same sense that there are 'finishing' schools.

4. Training for adult status

Social, moral and academic education are manifest functions of schools. The preparation of the young for a position in adult life is a latent function, not seen by many teachers or parents as part of the role of the former. Nevertheless, all teachers, in all schools, are involved in the process of allocation and selection, which, by giving different educations to different children, largely determines the jobs they will finally take and through this their adult status.

This can leave the children in the same social class as their parents, or involve them in upward or downward social mobility. At all levels, subject instruction, moral and social training must be given. The bright pupil from a poor home not only learns to pass examinations in the grammar school but learns the values and attitudes necessary for upward mobility. Similarly the academic failure is prepared for the low status which awaits him. Those who dissociate themselves from the work of the school are simultaneously insulating themselves from the pressures in society to be a success. There are still exceptions to this, for an outstanding personality, physical strength or beauty, social graces, ability to make an impact as singer or dancer on a stage, can still command an entry to occupations of high status, but the movement towards a meritocracy has been rapid. Further, children are probably aware of this process, at least in the secondary school. Thus in a study of grammar and secondary modern schools in London boys aged thirteen to fourteen years were shown to have a thorough understanding of our social class system.[12] Middle class boys in secondary modern schools were aware of the limitations this placed on their future, while working class boys in grammar schools had high occupational hopes.

It has been a recurring theme in this book that the preparation for adult status goes on in formal assessing, streaming and selection, and that once early action is taken by the teachers to label a child, the opportunities given him serve to justify the label. The initially bright, cooperative or well mannered are continually rewarded, promoted and placed in positions of authority. At the other extreme are the 'grubbies', arriving at school from unfavourable backgrounds and falling farther behind every year as they experience little success and continual subordination. Economically, a concentration on the brightest was inevitable once industrial society required an educated *élite*. Since 1945, however, selective systems have been under attack because they waste too much talent, and concern has grown for under-privileged groups who are not benefiting from the expanded opportunities.

The growing importance of education as one avenue to occupational status is not, however, an indication that social mobility has increased with educational opportunity. Data collected in 1949 showed that there had been little change over three generations in Britain.[13] The effect of the Education Act of 1944 may have been to increase mobility, but more recent work on the relation between educational achievement and social background makes this doubtful.[14] Further, studies on the effects of material affluence on the living styles of workers, show that there has been no apparent movement towards middle class values.[15] The educational improvements since 1944 have not yet succeeded in denting significantly the patterns of social stratification.

Each of these educational ends is concerned with the future as well as the present. Schools need to help children acquire the knowledge, values and behaviour that are needed for positions in adult life and at the same time to sort children into these statuses. This largely determines the organization of schools. An important factor in this is the latent, hidden nature of allocation and the priority given to subject instruction. The formal organization of schools is a product of aims recognized by those now in authority and of traditions from the past. In both cases, priority has been given to preparation rather than allocation. The contemporary debate over educational opportunity in selection for schools, and within schools, marks the emergence of thinking about appropriate means to meet this new end of allocation. Even without any reorganization of the school system the debate over equality of opportunity in education is serving to make teachers aware of the power they wield.

The organizational means

One way of examining the methods used by schools to achieve their goals is to rely on the three major branches of organizational theory.[16] The Classical theory concentrated on the formal organization of the business firm and on scientific management to improve its efficiency. Its approach was rational, both in its theories on the best administrative structure and in its method of time-and-motion study and piece-rates of earning. Human Relations theories on the other hand focused on the way informal groups developed their own norms within the organization. Since the studies at the Hawthorne works of the Western Electric Company in Chicago from 1927 to 1932, social factors, particularly good human relations, have been seen as a way to efficient and contented work. Significantly this school of thought, headed by Elton Mayo, also included Kurt Lewin who was influential in the Lippitt and White experiments referred to earlier. Good human relations in the factory and democracy in the classroom were part of the same movement. Both were a reaction against the growth of totalitarian states in the 1930s. On Human Relations theory a school would work well if the social and psychological needs of its pupils were met. Affection, esteem and security would be more important than marks or certificates.

This theory has been widely used in this book. But the classical theory of motivation is also important. The success of the teaching machine has been cited to point out the absence of sufficient rewards for most children in most classrooms. The attitude to most teaching of F. W. Taylor, the founder of scientific management, would have been similar to that of Professor Skinner, the pioneer of linear programmed instruction, that is, horror at the gap in time between the work done and the reward received, or even its complete absence. Further, as schools get larger the principles of efficient administration become very relevant.

Modern organization theory incorporates items from both of these earlier approaches. It studies all forms of organization and their social setting. It concerns itself with informal and formal structure. It studies the social as well as the material determinants of motivation. It recognizes the inevitability of conflicts occurring between groups, between the individual and the organization, and between traditions and the drive for efficiency. It recognizes that conflict serves to bring tensions into the open and hence promotes the necessary changes.

The formal organization of the school

A successful school has solved two sets of problems. First it has achieved the goals for which it was set up, or which have emerged since, and has continually adapted to external demands as these have changed. Secondly, it has integrated staff and pupils into a community in which there is a minimum of tension. Goal achievement, adaptation to extrenal changes, tension management within, and integration of its members, are all related fields, all necessary in this success. The main aim is to expose children to the maximum influence from teachers. The formal organization aims to accomplish this, but for success energy has to be directed into all four fields.

This can be illustrated by the example of a large junior school which abandoned streaming. This was an adaptation to external changes. As the evidence and pressure against streaming was felt by the school, the head discussed the issue with staff, finally deciding to work without streams for a year. The staff were divided and as difficulties arose in September, those against the change tried to get the experiment dropped. Neither staff nor children were used to the amount of group and individual work involved in teaching classes with a wide spread of ability. At this stage, too, reorganized classes tended to be discontented. Groups of friends were divided in the reshuffling of streamed classes. Parents were critical and the standard of work seemed to fall. The cohesion of the school as a community, its morale and the success of its teaching were threatened. However, the teething troubles lessened as staff got used to new methods and classes developed a sense of unity. While there was still opposition at the end of the year, the majority of the staff wanted the experiment to continue. The top junior form, however, was now set for basic subjects, initiating a fresh round of problems.

This can be seen as a cycle of events, starting from adaptation to ensure continued achievement of goals. This in turn produced the rearrangement of internal relationships. Where organizations have sufficient resources, research can smooth the path for change. A firm launching a new product on to the market first tests the potential demand, and builds up a sales campaign, while its production and personnel departments investigate the likely impact on the organization of work and workers. Schools have not the resources, time or energy for such planning and the cycle of events may be disruptive. In this primary school the initial problems were solved by the efforts of individual teachers. Much of this was directed at building up the morale of the class, pacifying outraged parents and discussing mutual problems with colleagues. Staff meetings were frequent and the headteacher was busy around the school in the early stages, helping staff and children. In an unplanned way energy had been switched to dealing with internal, expressive problems of the relations between groups and individuals. The organization had to deal with these in order to achieve success in the more obvious field of academic work.

The structures through which an organization achieves its objectives will now be considered.[17]

1. Authority and power

All schools are arranged so that children feel the authority of staff as experts and models. This comes down from the headteacher through the hierarchy of staff, and is delegated to selected children. A teacher in the classroom has behind him the weight of higher professional authority at many levels. When the teacher instructs, he communicates knowledge accumulated over centuries. His actions are backed by other staff and the headteacher, and are insulated from outside interference. If he has to enforce obedience he has the backing of the hierarchy. He has the material, moral and legal support of the whole education system. In return, the teacher recognizes the authority of those above him. He is often not free to organize his syllabus, timetable or hours of work. His performance is assessed by his headteacher and by Her Majesty's Inspectors. His methods are continually being criticized and revised through research in which he is not involved. He is backed by the authority structure but simultaneously confined by it. If he refuses to obey the rules laid down by those above him in the structure he feels their power. Headteachers, inspectors and local authorities hold the key to promotion and can wield an array of official and informal influences to bring him into line.

Those higher up in the hierarchy are similarly restrained. Headteachers rely on local authorities and may be frustrated, even ignored, by them. Schools can be closed or their status changed against their wishes. Inspectors are bound up in a hierarchy with strict protocol. Local authorities can be subjected to degrees of influence and coercion by the Department of Education and Science, particularly through their financial dependence. The aim of this power structure is to increase the influence of the adult world over the child through the teacher. The provision of facilities, the search for new methods, the increasing time taken over educating teachers all have this in view.

2. *Communication*

Authority and power ultimately guarantee that pupils will be physically positioned to be taught by staff and will acknowledge their competence in this respect. But parallel to this there must be a communication system; indeed, through this authority is spread and power exerted. There are two directions, horizontal among pupils, or staff or heads of departments, and vertical from the headteacher down through a hierarchy to the pupils. The ideal structure is one in which there is a free flow of communication up, down and across. This creates the conditions under which all staff can co-ordinate their efforts and in which pupils know what is expected of them. Simultaneously, staff know what the pupils are thinking and the headteacher knows how his policies have been received.

Horizontal communication among equals not only helps solve problems and ensures common policies, but means that all can receive support. Junior staff can get advice from senior, methods can be synchronized, difficult children can be given consistent help. In small schools informal talks between staff usually suffice, provided no schisms develop. But in larger schools, communications can be blocked within departments or houses. The only channel for resolving difficulties is at staff meetings where the horizontal communication between staff is influenced by the presence of the head-teacher.

Vertical, hierarchical channels of communication are usually necessary to coordinate effort. But the hierarchy tends to block communication. Headteachers, senior assistants, heads of depart-ments and housemasters can sit on information going up or down. A school under a strong head can be perfectly coordinated, though junior staff may have instructions but little information. Blau and Scott, reviewing the evidence from experiments with small groups, conclude that hierarchical organization, by actually restricting the free flow of communication, improves the coordination of effort, but is unsuitable for solving fresh problems.[18] Further, there is a limit to the control over their activities that teachers, as professionals, will accept. Behind the closed doors of a classroom the united effort may be replaced by an entirely individual approach. Here the teacher's power is absolute.

This tendency for hierarchical organizations to be inflexible in the face of new problems results from the barriers on two-way com-munication. Orders come down but there is no feed-back from below. The headteacher is often unaware of changing conditions or new problems. His policies are amended by the teachers to meet these changes and coordination breaks down. Similarly teachers transmit information to, but more rarely receive it from, the pupils. Consequently they can organize efficiently, but cannot gauge their impact or the underground reaction.

The problem of allowing pupils a say in the running of the school hinges on this point of the inverse relation between coordination and communication in hierarchical structures. A hierarchy is inevitable because responsibility rests with the headteacher and his staff. They initiate and implement policy. Channels for pupils to express their views must either be confined to matters outside the central purposes of the school, or used primarily as a safety valve. A school is an organization for adults to influence the young. This defines the limits of democracy, for children's views can never be allowed to disrupt this relation. Progressive schools may be skilful enough to gain the willing cooperation of pupils, but the very act of doing so is a triumph of hierarchically organized staff effort.

The barriers to communication in a school occur at all levels. Headteachers, senior assistants, departmental heads, assistant teachers, prefects, monitors and pupils receive and transmit information, but each tends to know less than those above and more than those below. The greater the barriers, the less will those below appreciate why orders are being given. They will not see the orders as reasonable and will tend to question the need for them. Consequently, staff or prefects must wield more power to get their way. Recognition of the rights of others to be obeyed depends on the subordinates receiving sufficient information. Committees, notices, informal chats, school councils, periods reserved for discussing mutual problems, not only help pass information but promote authority and good relations. Similarly Parent–Teacher Associations by improving communication can also increase the support for the school.

3. *Rewards*

A school must also be organized to motivate everyone through adequate rewards. This, too, works parallel with the structure of power and authority. Among the staff responsibility allowances differentiate levels in the hierarchy. But more important are the privileges and symbols attached to particular statuses. These give staff and pupils prestige and praise for carrying out vital responsibilities. Failure to reward in this way weakens the motivation to carry out the tasks and finally leads to resentment at being asked at all. The domestic science mistress does not like it to be taken for granted that she will always arrange for tea at staff meetings. The milk monitors miss going out to play at break. Perceptive headteachers always give public praise for extra duties cheerfully performed. Class teachers not only thank the monitors, but make it clear how valuable this service is.

Again, the larger the school and the more consolidated the hierarchy within it, the more barriers there are to an efficient system of rewards. The headmistress in a junior school can see the extra effort put in by her colleagues, but the non-teaching head of a large school only learns of this at second-hand. Blocked communications may stop rewards being given, or given to the right people. Further, like communications, rewarding is a two-way process. The volunteers in a class are not only given thanks and privileges, but their reason for volunteering is frequently their admiration for the teacher. They grant him prestige, he rewards them. A teacher starts a club after school which brings it esteem, and he is rewarded by the headteacher.

The most important aspect of the system of rewards is to motivate in the classroom. The rewards may be instrumental or expressive, but must be carefully arranged to cover all the children. Some may work hard to keep at the top of the form, others to please the teacher. Some may be looking forward to passing an examination, others to keeping in the group in which they feel secure. All will need rewarding, some tangibly, some emotionally.

4. Informal and external influences

These formal structures of authority and power, communication and reward, provide a framework for the work in the classroom. They are the prerequisites of an efficient school, the base from which good teaching can develop. But each is mirrored by an informal structure modifying its effects. Children have their own leaders, often opposing school policy. Individual members of staff become alternative centres of influence. The larger the school, the longer the chain of command from headteacher to pupil, the more opportunities there are for these informal centres of power to become autonomous. Each unofficial leader can organize support among his followers and reward them. Indeed, the expressive rewards in children's groups often outweigh the instrumental rewards offered by the school, resulting in waste of talent, early leaving and discipline problems.

Informal communications also accompany official information. Rumours fly round the staffroom. Children, guessing at reasons for a change in routine, soon share common interpretations. The grapevine enables children to support each other against the staff. Informal norms grow through this communication. Just as factory workers go slow or work to rule, so can children. Norms are established which oppose official rules.

Similarly formal organization is affected by external influences. The authority of the teacher is reduced or increased according to the level of parental support, the direction of pull in the social background of the children and their involvement in this, compared with the school. The prestige of teachers in a school also depends on their prestige in the community. Communications flow into the school at all levels and influence those which have been generated within it. The organization of a school may be designed to maximize the exposure of children to the influence of the staff, but it works alongside informal influences and in a wider environmental context.

Throughout this chapter, the increasing size of schools has been shown to produce new problems. This is most marked in the need for new administrative structure. Headteachers inevitably become administrators. There is a need for more committees, more clearly defined areas of responsibility, more written communication. Yet administrative skills are not usually part of the armoury with which teachers are equipped by training.[19] Consequently there is a tendency for schools to expand without setting up the administrative machinery which will eliminate or reduce the inevitable tensions. In these circumstances, instead of the school having a single goal, individual teachers or groups of colleagues establish their own goals and their own individual ways of meeting them. The children are exposed to different and often conflicting influences and the education they receive is inconsistent.

10

Conclusions

The main object of this book has been to give a sociologist's view of the school. As a discipline, sociology is always probing below the surface of social life to uncover hidden motives. It is the ideal subject for those who are always asking 'why' and 'how' about human behaviour. Inevitably, therefore, sociological analysis tends to concentrate on those areas where behaviour or belief either result from underlying factors not at first apparent, or where there is a discrepancy between these and other areas of activity. The sociologist is usually found at work where there are problems rather than where things are going smoothly. Further, he is never just describing what he sees, but is trying to explain it.

His subject matter is not individuals as persons, but the roles they play and the groups they form. This is what he is observing and testing. Underlying these he detects the norms that largely determine individual and group behaviour. Finally he assesses the values that these norms serve. This inevitably involves some analysis of the historical origins and evolution of values and norms. At all four levels of the concepts of role, groups, norms and values he has to be concerned with the past as well as the present, because values and norms once established, tend to persist long after the conditions in which they originated have changed.

The use of concepts means that sociologists speak the same language, and discipline themselves within the same framework as their colleagues. This not only enables them to use the accumulated work of others, but means that each contribution can rest on previous work and prepare for the next. A common language and shared concepts are essential not only for communication but for the knowledge gained to be cumulative. This is the reason why a subject dealing with everyday, concrete activity is often written in such an abstract language. This is part of the attempt to get below the level of surface description to establish logical connections which explain the behaviour. The sociologist uses the concepts to classify and establish laws connecting the facts he has observed.

But this subject discipline also applies to the methods used. The sociologist tries to control his own prejudices and to become a detached observer. He uses established methods of procedure in his investigations so that others can assess the reliability of his results. In this way his work can be used as a spring-board for further research. As ideas about human action come to mind, the sociologist is fitting them into existing knowledge and formulating hypotheses for testing them in practice. At all stages there is a discipline into which his strategy fits.

This approach means that the sociologist, while attracted to the subject by his interest in human behaviour, tries to remain dispassionate while he is investigating it. Inevitably his own personal prejudices affect his choice of subject, the methods chosen and even the interpretation of his results. But he is not primarily concerned with evaluating behaviour, only analysing it. Comprehensive education may be good or bad, but the sociological investigations which have been used in the debate, have concentrated on uncovering the educational and social effects of selection. Those concerned were probably drawn to the subject through a feeling that selection was wrong in principle, but their work should have been free of this evaluation, through the discipline of their subject.

Consequently, readers of this, as of any sociological text, may ask 'Whose side is the author on?' The answer is that as a sociologist he is neutral. He may be attracted to a particular subject because he feels deeply about it, but this should not influence his methods of analysis. But the analysis of social groupings such as schools, produces insights which can be used to make them more efficient. More important, these enable the individuals concerned in these groupings to detect the determinants of their own behaviour, and consequently provide the opportunity for exercising more personal freedom. Knowledge of the forces which have produced the values and norms that determine the roles played by an individual and those with whom he interacts, enable him to assert his independence.

Knowing how the school works as a social organization brings power to control it, to make teaching more effective.

The structural-functional, conflict and organization models used in this study focused not on individuals, but on the roles played, the relation between these and the forces defining, teaching, arranging and enforcing them. It is the roles which are the permanent, detectable and predictable elements in the school, and consequently of most interest to the sociologist. Schools are primarily agencies for teaching adult roles to children. Through all the perspectives run two themes related to this purpose which largely determine the influence and social structure of the schools. These are the concentration of influences on staff and pupils to internalize values and norms, and secondly, the institutionalization which arranges these influences and the roles they define, into patterns of behaviour.[1]

Internalization

All schools exert pressures on those involved to accept values and norms as their own. They become part of a culture which they internalize. The official organization tries to gain control over this. Staff try to expose children to those values that are considered appropriate for contemporary adult life. They lay down rules of acceptable or unacceptable behaviour. At the same time, informal influences may be promoting other values and external influences are affecting the responses to both. Children are exposed to staff and peer influence inside the school and are pressed towards one or the other by family or community pressures.

Regardless of the relative strength of these influences, schools are designed to promote learning in this moral, social sense as well as in academic work. Routine and order govern the school day. The child is surrounded by desks, books and apparatus. Teachers stress a common moral line and insist on the appropriate behaviour. Most parents continue this policy and extend the pressure over more of the child's day. Opposing these are informal influences originating among the children, often reinforced from outside in the community or home. But although these may conflict with the school, they add another pressure on the individual child. These all add up to a situation of constraint. Similarly teachers are subject to internal and external pressures which define their role.

It would be difficult for anyone to remain insulated from the press of the norms. They define the patterns of behaviour in the school, and are backed by sanctions, whether from the staff or other children. Involvement in the working and social life of the school brings psychological satisfactions. These may be expressive, instrumental or moral. Emotional needs are met through friendship in small groups and in organized activity. The school can provide the qualifications needed in adult life and satisfy a thirst for knowledge. The moral codes of the school can provide the security of knowing what is right and wrong. The involvement may be in both the informal and formal life of the school, or in one but not the other. But in every case, the needs for friendship, affection and security are met through the individual accepting controls on his behaviour. As the slang, the signals, the symbols and the secrets are learnt, so are the norms. The difficult children also have these psychological needs. The school contains groups in which these can be satisfied. But this also means that they are simultaneously exposed to the influences and sanctions that the school can bring to bear. Complete insulation from these is unlikely.

This is not only a form of social contract, an exchange of freedom of action and thought for the satisfactions of belonging. Nor is it only the individual surrounded by social pressures to conform. The internalization of values and norms occurs mainly as a consequence of being given a status and in playing the accompanying role.[2] A child enters a school in which his position and behaviour have been predetermined. But in acting this role as pupil, he comes to accept it as his own. The new pupil takes on the attitudes and behaviour of a first former as he plays the role. But this has been defined without reference to him. Nevertheless he internalizes it as he plays the part. In Berger's terms 'one becomes wise by being appointed a professor, believing by engaging in activities that presuppose belief, and ready for battle by marching in formation'.[3] One achieves professional authority through practising teaching and children become responsible adults through being given more and more responsibility as they grow older. But they can also become delinquent by being more and more involved in groups whose norms flout authority.

A school then, by allocating staff and pupils their statuses, by providing the external trappings of status and the norms which define behaviour, aids the internalization of the characteristics of these roles. The influence of a school is determined by the success of these arrangements. As agencies of socialization they are engaged in preparing children for adult life. The internalization of school norms is an important means through which this occurs.

Institutionalization

This analysis of the school started with the observation that random movement in the playground changes into predictable patterns on entry to the school. This indicates that the interaction within school is institutionalized. Not only have those involved internalized the norms, but also the promise of rewards for good behaviour, and the penalties for non-conformity. This results in shared prescriptions for action and expectations for the future, which produce the patterns of behaviour. This ordering of social relations, or institutionalization, accompanies internalization.[4] Norms must be accepted before pupils are motivated to follow the patterns. Similarly the behaviour of staff is confined within limits which they too accept, because the limits too have been internalized in the process of becoming teachers. Further, all those involved in a school come to accept part at least of the total normative pattern, in addition to that which relates only to their status. Both staff and pupils recognize that each is playing a role which is legitimate. Children accept that teachers have to act in certain ways, and staff recognize norms established among pupils. All are bound by common codes and customs.

This institutionalization is not confined to behaviour. A school is not only notable for its ordered movement and interactions. Many children and staff come to think of it as their school, a unique and worthwhile place, to which they give their loyalty. They are rewarded by the warmth which is felt in such a community. Those who do not share these feelings are denied the rewards of belonging and have to seek these elsewhere. Institutionalization is, therefore, a process through which beliefs as well as behaviour come to be predictable. When a new infant class first meets, it has little in common. Its behaviour is haphazard, unregulated and governed by a variety of standards. 'Don't wriggle about', 'Be a brave boy', 'You're being a silly girl', 'Don't sulk', express these underlying standards and are backed, if necessary, by further action which guides the children into approved channels. Slowly beliefs and behaviour are institutionalized as the children internalize the values and norms of the class. Within a short time the disorder of the early days is transformed. Standards, regulations and interactions fall into distinct patterns, felt to be natural by all in the class and impressive in their order to the outsider.

This affects staff as well as children. Just as the new pupil adjusts to the demands of the school, until he fits into the informal and formal arrangements, so the teacher has to adapt. From the early days of experimentation there is a steady adjustment to balance the often contradictory demands for high academic standards from children of different abilities and attitudes, for order and friendly relations in the classroom, for objectivity in assessment, and allowance for individual differences. The teacher establishes a routine which enables a balance to be maintained between these demands. 'It is further noted that some typical modes of adaptation were made by teachers over a period of years as they routinized their functions in such a way as to minimize the amount of personal stress which they experienced in a situation of continuous conflict.'[5]

This tendency for routines to develop as standards are developed indicates a degree of integration between behaviour and belief. Children not only tend to conform, but also to see this as right. Young children can be outraged when an interesting lesson is interrupted. Similarly, they can be upset by changes in routine and these are often introduced by promises that the innovations will be exciting. Further, teachers plan in order to avoid disrupting the pattern of social relations in the class. Sociometry developed as a means of ensuring this compatibility of working groups. This care is necessary, for once established, social relations acquire a degree of sanctity. A class develops unwritten, but powerful rules, governing its social structure. Anyone, including the teacher, who breaks these rules, violates feelings of right and wrong. Just as those who disgrace the school in public are punished not so much for the offence as for the wrong they have done to the school, so upsetting the normative structure of the school class can be seen as morally outrageous.

A school, however, is never completely harmonious. Discord may be institutionalized. A class may be basically orderly, but part of this order is not intended by the teacher, nor educationally desirable. There will be individuals who are ignored, laughed at or bullied. Norms of work may be low. The teacher's freedom of action is narrowly defined, so that he accepts less work and more noise than his ideal, and exerts less moral influence than he would like. But this, too, comes to be accepted as part of the pattern of the school day. It is institutionalized, and attempts to set more work, get complete silence or tighten up on the behaviour of the class outside the formroom are not playing the game. 'Who does he think he is' is a common response to a teacher whose actions, reasonable in the light of the official definition of his role, violate what has come to be seen as reasonable practice.

But under the surface, outside the range of staff supervision there is the institutionalization of unofficial values, regulations and practices. Pupils come to accept sexual experimentation, smoking, swearing and the rejection of the school values. They are subject to punishments and rewards within their peer groups and are expected to conform rigidly to their behaviour patterns. Here is an integrated system, established horizontally between equals, underneath the vertical system linking staff and children, and giving an alternative and often very powerful blueprint.

Finally, where these differences between the policies of the school and the informal patterns among the pupils spill over into conflict, this, too, is institutionalized. In Chapter 5, the tendency for rules to develop, defining the way the struggle is conducted, was described. This, too, is a pattern into which behaviour is channelled and regulated. Each side goes so far and no further. Each has its own ideas on the lengths to which the other can go. But again, both sides share a common recognition of this institution of conflict.

There is a shared normative order even here, whether governing actual strife between staff and pupils, or defining the apathy into which the differences have congealed.

The degree of institutionalization, the power of the constraints on individual action, vary with the importance of the activity. In the playground, the children may behave in a random haphazard way, but the nearer the classroom, the more predictable is the behaviour. A junior class may be allowed to work without close supervision at times and to wander into the by-ways of subjects, but as examinations approach, the seniors are kept rigidly to the syllabus. The school assembly, right at the centre of its life, is not only tightly organized, but supported and solemnized by religion. Further, misbehaviour here is morally outrageous and heavily punished. The more vital the activity is to the work of the school, the tighter is the institutionalization.

The strength with which the norms press decreases, rather as the field of a bar magnet weakens as distance from it increases. In the headteacher's study a child may be solemn and impressed. But once among his friends in the playground, resolutions are forgotten and the head's moralizing is laughed at. The integration of values, regulations and action is never complete and many remain on the margins, never fully committed, always attracted elsewhere. This is why the power of the school to improve morals and social behaviour is limited. It is one magnet among many and its field of influence can be weakened, as well as reinforced, by other agencies. Institutionalization can be visualized as the formation of the patterns of these lines of force. This has been shown to occur not only in the official life of the school, but also among informal cliques and in the conflict between groups. These are fields which exert contrary pulls, thus limiting the power of the school to promote its aims.

This coexistence of institutionalized patterns is rarely a source of tension for individual children. They switch from one code to another without difficulty. But at all times the situation is defined for them. They know how to behave and what standards to adopt in a variety of circumstances, and can switch instantaneously from one to another as these change. Only rarely is there a situation in which this learning fails to provide a framework for understanding and action. Staff serving the children at the Christmas dinner are a rare example where neither knows how to behave. Both feel awkward because the culture has defined the roles for the reverse of this situation and can give no guidance. Staff laugh it off and retire afterwards, feeling very relieved that this comes only once a year.

Internalization and institutionalization between them, therefore, promote individual security and structural stability. Staff and pupils know what is expected from them and the school remains orderly. But this is not necessarily the equilibrium which was intended by the staff or educationally desirable. Many schools are inert and some are locked in perpetual tension.

It is in this routinized context that new teaching methods, curriculum revision, and attempts at reorganization have to fit. Schools are established social organizations. They can absorb, distort, modify or annul new influences. Unless this is accounted for in the strategy of innovation, the results will not be those anticipated. The stability of schools is not in itself good or bad, for it can stop innovation and preserve the bad as well as the good. What is often seen as spontaneous behaviour can be a part of an intricate pattern in which the participants have a vested interest in stopping change.

But the social organization of the school does more than provide a framework within which education must be accommodated. The statuses to which pupils are allocated, whether by staff or by other pupils, determine both their performance and opportunities in school, and later in adult life. The roles are not determined by those playing them but by the prevailing norms. Although individuals can exercise personal initiative within these definitions, they are affected first by their actions being socially sanctioned, and secondly by the expectation of others that they will abide by the role definitions. The school may educate to obtain a consciously planned result, but its social organization also acts to influence the personality and performance of children, and this is often unrecognized and uncontrolled. This can cause anxiety among teachers, who tend to accept personal responsibility for problems which may be determined by the institutional character of the school.

It is within schools that children rehearse roles which they will later perform as men and women, husbands and wives, fathers and mothers, workers, voters, neighbours and citizens. The school sets the stage to accord with current intellectual, moral and social ideas of these roles, but backstage unofficial influences give other versions. Each is backed by other influences in the community. The school is, therefore, not only the organized agent of socialization, it is the social setting wherein children must meet and resolve the often conflicting models available for them to copy.

Notes

Chapter 1: The school in society

1 Li An-Che, 'Zuni. Some observations and queries', *Am. Anthropologist*, vol. 39, 1937, pp. 62–76, maintains that among the Pueblo Indians informal education is more pervasive and disciplined than formal schooling.

2 M. H. Watkins, 'The West African bush school', in G. Spindler, *Education and Culture*, New York, Holt, Rinehart and Winston, 1965, pp. 426–43. For the place of such schools in the life of a society, see H. A. Stayt, *The Bavenda*, Oxford U.P., 1931 or S. F. Nadel, *A Black Byzantium*, Oxford U.P., 1942.

3 C. W. M. Hart, 'Contracts between prepubertal and postpubertal education', in Spindler, *op. cit.*, pp. 400–25. Hart argues that the relaxed instruction for the young child gives way to tough, intensive methods to ensure correct moral and social behaviour.

4 M. Mead, 'Our educational emphases in primitive perspective', in Spindler, *op. cit.*, p. 316.

5 M. Herskovits, *Man and his Works*, New York, A. A. Knopf, 1948, p. 314. G. A. Pettitt, 'Primitive education in North America', Univ. of California Publications in *American Archaeology and Ethnology*, vol. 43, 1, 1946, pp. 1–182 shows how conflict is reduced by using outsiders to perform unpleasant tasks in the training of children to avoid harming the solidarity of the group.

6 J. W. Adamson, *English Education*, Cambridge U.P. 1930, pp. 204–5. See also D. V. Glass, 'Education and social change in modern Britain', in A. H. Halsey, J. Floud and C. A. Anderson, *Education, Economy and Society*, New York, Free Press, 1961, pp. 391–413.

7 *Higher Education* (Robbins Report), H.M.S.O., 1, p. 68.

8 For Higher Horizons, see M. Mayer, *The Schools*, Bodley Head, 1961, pp. 130–4. See also, G. Graham, *The Public School in the American Community*, New York, Harper and Row, 1963, pp. 300–1. This book also has information on other community programmes.

For Head Start, see 'Fact sheet on project Head Start', *Congressional*

Quarterly Inc., 18 March 1966, pp. 615–16. See also Annual Reports of the Office of Economic Opportunity, U.S.A.

9 P. Drucker, *Landmarks of Tomorrow*, Heinemann, 1959, p. 87.

10 H. Schelsky, 'Family and school in modern society', in Halsey *et al.*, *op. cit.*, p. 417.

11 *Half our Future* (Newsom), Report of the Central Advisory Council for Education (England), H.M.S.O., 1963, p. 72.

12 See R. L. Archer, *Secondary Education in the Nineteenth Century*, Cambridge U.P., 1921. For changes in the previous century, see N. Hans, *New Trends in Education in the 18th Century*, Routledge and Kegan Paul, 1951.

13 B. Wilson, 'The teacher's role – a sociological analysis', *Brit. Jrn. Soc.*, vol. XIII, 1962, pp. 15–32.

14 D. Williams, *The Preceptor's Assistant*, London, 1819, p. 84.

15 See any writings by M. Mead on education, particularly, 'Thinking ahead: Why is education obsolete?', *Harvard Business Rev.*, vol. 36, Nov., Dec., 1958, pp. 23–30. See also 'The School in American culture', in Halsey *et al.*, *op. cit.*, pp. 421–33.

16 R. Linton, *The Tree of Culture*, New York, A. A. Knopf, 1955, p. 11.

Chapter 2: The culture of the school

1 J. Wilson, *Public Schools and Private Practice*, Allen and Unwin, 1962, p. 56.

2 P. W. Musgrave, *The Sociology of Education*, Methuen, 1965, p. 224.

3 These modes of action were developed in T. Parsons, *The Social System*, New York, Free Press, 1951. Two useful secondary sources on this rather difficult book are C. P. Loomis, *Modern Social Theories*, New Jersey, Van Nostrand, 1965, particularly pp. 327–441 and H. C. Bredemeier and R. M. Stephenson, *The Analysis of Social Systems*, New York, Holt, Rinehart and Winston, 1962.

4 J. J. Rousseau, *Emile* (1762), Dent, 1955.

5 The author was responsible for supervising students in schools of all types. The exercises were designed to get them to see the school as a social organization.

6 See T. W. Moore, 'The trouble with school', *University of London, Inst. of Ed. Bull.*, vol. 9, Summer, 1966, pp. 19–21.

7 These terms and ideas are taken from E. Goffman, *The Presentation of Self in Everyday Life*, University of Edinburgh, Soc. Sci. Res. Centre, 1958. See also *Asylums*, New York, Anchor, 1961.

8 *Children and their Primary Schools* (Plowden), Report of the Central Advisory Council for Education (England), H.M.S.O. 1967, p. 37.

9 *Early Leaving*, Report of the Central Advisory Council for Education (England), H.M.S.O., 1954. See also, *15 to 18* (Crowther), Report of the Central Advisory Council for Education (England), H.M.S.O., 1959, pp. 6–10. H. Davies, *Culture and the Grammar School*, Routledge and Kegan Paul, 1965, Ch. 2, pp. 19–35, shows how this affects the schools.

10 The concepts of manifest and latent functions were developed by R. K. Merton, *Social Theory and Social Structure*, New York, Free Press, 1957.

11 For examples of what he terms the 'Underground', see J. Wilson, *op. cit.*, pp. 103–7.

12 See H. C. Bredemeier and R. M. Stephenson, *op. cit.*

13 C. Dilke, *Dr Moberly's Mint Mark*, Heinemann, 1965, pp. 92–100.

Chapter 3: The social structure of the school

1 See J. Berger, *Invitation to Sociology*, Penguin, 1966, pp. 81–171, and particularly pp. 116–19.

2 C. Lacey, 'Some sociological concomitants of academic streaming in a grammar school', *Brit. Jrn Soc.*, Vol. XVIII, 3, Sept. 1966, pp. 245–62.

3 D. H. Hargreaves, *Social Relations in a Secondary School*, Routledge and Kegan Paul, 1967.

4 See B. Jackson, *Streaming: an Education System in Miniature*, Routledge and Kegan Paul, 1964. See also, J. W. B. Douglas, *The Home and School*, MacGibbon and Kee, 1964.

5 E. Haufmann, 'Social structure of a group of kindergarten children', in W. W. Charters and N. L. Gage, *Readings in the Social Psychology of Education*, New York, Allyn and Bacon, 1963, pp. 123–5.

6 W. A. L. Blyth, 'Sociometric study of children's groups in English schools', *Brit. Jrn. Ed. Studies*, May 1960, pp. 138–9.

7 W. Gordon, *The Social System of the High School*, Ill., The Free Press, 1957, pp. 79–98.

8 J. Coleman, *The Adolescent Society*, Ill., The Free Press, 1960.

9 H. S. Becker, 'The teacher in the authority system of the public school', in A. Etzioni, *Complex Organizations*, New York, Holt, Rinehart and Winston, 1965, p. 246.

10 B. Wilson, *op. cit.*

11 J. Gabriel, *An Analysis of the Emotional Problems of the Teacher in the Classroom*, Melbourne, F. W. Cheshire, 1957, p. 68.

12 W. Taylor, *The Secondary Modern School*, Faber, 1963.

13 W. A. L. Blyth, *English Primary Education*, Routledge and Kegan Paul, 1965, pp. 75–6.

14 J. Webb, 'The Sociology of a School,' *Brit. Jrn. of Soc.*, vol. 13, 1962, pp. 264–72.

15 D. H. Hargreaves, *op. cit.*

16 W. A. L. Blyth, 1960, *op. cit.*

17 O. A. Oeser, *Teacher, Pupil and Task*, Tavistock Pbns, 1955, p. 7.

18 *Children and Their Primary Schools* (Plowden), pp. 395–400.

19 C. H. Zoeftig, 'What's happened to discipline at school?' *Where*, vol. 9, Summer 1962, p. 5.

20 K. Mannheim and W. A. C. Stewart, *An Introduction to the Sociology of Education*, Routledge and Kegan Paul, 1962, p. 136.

21 *Half our Future* (Newsom), pp. 87–97. See also *Schools Council*, H.M.S.O., Working Paper No. 2, 1965, pp. 22–3 and 31–4.

22 D. E. M. Gardner and J. E. Cross, *The Role of the Teacher in the Infant and Nursery School*, Pergamon, 1965, p. 171.

23 R. G. Barker and P. V. Gump, *Big School, Small School*, Stanford, Stanford U.P., 1964.

24 S. Marshall, *An Experiment in Education*, Cambridge U.P., 1963, p. 27.

Chapter 4: Socialization and social control

1 University of Birmingham, Institute of Education, Training College Research Group, *The Probationary Year*, 1965.

2 T. W. Moore, *op. cit.* (ch. 2.6).

3 L. Ridgway and I. Lawton, *Family Grouping in the Infants' School*, Ward Lock, 1965, p. 15.

4 *Children and their Primary Schools* (Plowden), p. 136. See also pp. 135–59 for the reasons behind this recommendation.

5 See for example, B. Jackson and D. Marsden, *Education and the Working Class*, Routledge and Kegan Paul, 1962, p. 95.

6 Examples of these methods can be found in Blyth (ch. 3.5), pp. 139–40 and in *Children and their Primary Schools* (Plowden), p. 162.

7 J. Jones, 'Social class and the under fives', *New Society*, no. 221, 22 Dec. 1966, pp. 935–6.

8 C. Hindley, 'Ability and social class', *The Listener*, 31 March 1966, pp. 464–6.

9 R. K. Merton, *Social Theory and Social Structure*, Ill., The Free Press, 1957, pp. 131–60. A discussion of the theories of subcultural delinquency which derive from these ideas can be found in D. Downes, *The Delinquent Solution*, Routledge and Kegan Paul, 1966, pp. 1–99.

10 C. Lacey, (ch. 3.2), D. H. Hargreaves, (ch. 3.3).

11 'Balaam', *Chalk in my Hair*, Benn, 1953, pp. 10–11.

12 E. Goffman (ch. 2.7).

13 *Ibid.*

Chapter 5: Schools as centres of conflict

1 N. A. Flanders and S. Havumaki, 'Group compliance to dominative teacher influence', in W. W. Charters and N. L. Gage (ch. 3.4), pp. 162–72.

2 *Half our Future* (Newsom), pp. 14–15.

3 M. P. Carter, *Education, Employment and Leisure*, Pergamon, 1963, p. 23.

4 *Half our Future*, pp. 21–2.

5 *Children and their Primary Schools* (Plowden), pp. 50–68.

6 W. Waller, *The Sociology of Teaching*, New York, J. Wiley, 1965, p. 10. This book is an outstanding contribution to the sociology of the school from the conflict viewpoint.

7 R. Farley, *Secondary Modern Discipline*, A. and C. Black, 1960, p. 50.

8 *The Guardian*, 3 Dec. 1966.

9 J. Webb (ch. 3.13), p. 264.

10 W. Waller, *op. cit.*, p. 10.

11 N. J. Smelser, *Theory of Collective Behaviour*, Routledge and Kegan Paul, 1962.

12 *Half our Future*, pp. 194–233.

13 E. K. Wickman, *Children's Behaviour and Teacher's Attitudes*, New York, The Commonwealth Fund, 1928. J. Gabriel, *op. cit.*

14 W. Waller, *op. cit.* p. 196.

15 *Half our Future*, p. 2.

16 *Ibid.* p. 23.

17 J. B. Mays, *Education and the Urban Child*, Liverpool U.P., 1962, pp. 82–9.

18 D. H. Hargreaves (ch. 3.3).

19 W. Waller, *op. cit.* p. 12.

20 C. Booth, *Life and Labour of the People in London*, London, 1892, p. 211. G. A. N. Lowndes, *The Silent Social Revolution*, Oxford U.P., 1937, pp. 179–80. J. B. Mays, *op. cit.*, pp. 87–8.

21 R. Dahrendorf, *Class and Class Conflict in Industrial Society*, Routledge and Kegan Paul, 1959, pp. 206–7.
22 J. S. Mill, *On Liberty* (1859), Dent, 1944, pp. 65–170.
23 G. Lyons, 'Primary school', *New Society*, No. 207, 15 Sept. 1966, p. 396.
24 See D. Downes, *op. cit.*, pp. 236–41 for a discussion of this.
25 See R. H. Wilkinson, *The Prefects: British Leadership and the Public School Tradition*, Oxford U.P., 1964.
26 *Malvern Gazette*, 29 Dec. 1966, p. 10.
27 W. A. L. Blyth (ch. 3.6), vol. 11, pp. 58–64.
28 M. Mayer (ch. 1.8), pp. 143–4.
29 A. Inkeles, *What is Sociology?*, New Jersey, Prentice-Hall, 1965, pp. 28–46 has a useful discussion of models. See also, R. Dahrendorf, *op cit.*, pp. 157–65. Also, D. Lockwood, 'Some Remarks on the "Social System" ', *Brit. Jrn. Soc.*, vol. VII, 2, 1956.

Chapter 6: Order and discipline

1 See A. Etzioni, *A Comparative Analysis of Complex Organizations*, Ill.,The Free Press, 1961. For a shorter version of this see A. Etzioni, *Modern Organizations*, New Jersey, Prentice-Hall, 1964, pp. 58–74.
2 N. E. Cutts and N. Moseley, *Teaching the Disorderly Pupil*, Longmans, 1957, p. 3.
3 *Ibid*, p. 6.
4 M. E. Highfield and A. Pinsent, *A Survey of Rewards and Punishments*, Newnes, 1962, p. 162.
5 A. Etzioni, *A Comparative Analysis of Complex Organizations*, pp. 45–6.
6 B. Foss, 'Punishments, rewards and the child', *New Society*, 9 Sept. 1965, No. 154, pp. 8–10.
7 See J. B. Mays (ch. 5.17).
8 B. Bernstein, 'Social factors in educational achievement', in A. H. Halsey *et al.*, (ch. 1.6), pp. 288–314.
9 J. Gabriel (ch. 3.11), pp. 76–119.
10 A Schoolteacher, 'Neighbourhood School', *New Society*, 23 June 1966, No. 195, pp. 9–13.
11 M. E. Highfield and A. Pinsent, *op. cit.*, p. 280.
12 *Half our Future*, pp. 63–4.
13 *Children and their Primary Schools*, p. 270.
14 G. A. N. Lowndes (ch. 5.20), p. 17.
15 E. K. Wickman (ch. 5.13), p. 116.

16 M. E. Highfield and A. Pinsent, *op. cit.*, p. 164.

17 *Ibid.*, p. 162.

18 *Ibid.*, p. 163.

19 M. Mayer (ch. 1.8), pp. 142–3.

20 National Education Association, 'Teacher opinion on pupil behaviour', *Research Bull.*, vol. 34, No. 2, April 1956.

21 M. P. Carter (ch. 5.3), p. 22.

22 R. K. White and R. Lippitt, see 8.1.

23 M. Atkinson, *Junior School Community*, Longmans, 1962, p. 54.

24 A. B. Clegg, 'The Role of the School', in *Delinquency and Discipline*, 'Education' pamphlet, Councils and Education Press, 1963, pp. 15–16.

Chapter 7: The authority of the teacher

1 W. Waller (ch. 5.6), page 189.

2 M. Weber, *The Theory of Social and Economic Organization*, New York, The Free Press, 1964, pp. 324–92.

3 M. Weber, *ibid.*, footnote by T. Parsons, pp. 58–60.

4 G. A. N. Lowndes (ch. 5.20), pp. 14–15.

5 J. Banfield, C. Bowyer and E. Wilkie, 'Parents and Education', *Ed. Res.*, vol. 9, No. 1, Nov. 1966, pp. 63–6.

6 J. W. B. Douglas (ch. 3.4), p. 155.

7 *Children and their Primary Schools* (Plowden), pp. 34–6.

8 B. Wilson (ch. 1.13), p. 31.

9 *Ibid.*, pp. 18–19.

10 B. Bernstein, 'Social factors in educational achievement', in A. H. Halsey *et al.* (ch. 1.6), p. 304.

11 B. Wilson (ch. 3.13), p. 21.

12 M. Burn, *Mr Lyward's Answer*, Hamish Hamilton, 1956, p. 128.

13 A. S. Neill, 'What shortage?', *Times Ed. Supp.* No. 2694, 6 Jan. 1967, p. 33.

14 K. Mannheim and W. A. C. Stewart, *An Introduction to the Sociology of Education*, Routledge and Kegan Paul, 1962, pp. 138–42. See also W. Waller, (ch. 5.6), pp. 189–211.

Chapter 8: Classroom climate, activity and style of teaching

1 H. H. Anderson *et al.*, *Studies of Teachers' Classroom Personalities*, *I*, *II*, *III* (Applied Psychology Monographs), Stanford, Stanford U.P., 1945 and 1946.

2 R. K. White and R. Lippitt, *Autocracy and Democracy*, New York, Harper, 1960. See also, E. E. Maccoby, T. Newcomb and E. L. Hartley, *Readings in Social Psychology*, Methuen, pp. 496–511. For a critique of these experiments, see R. C. Anderson, 'Learning in discussion: A resumé of the authoritarian – democratic studies', in W. W. Charters and N. L. Gage, *op. cit.*, pp. 153–62.

3 C. M. Fleming, *Teaching – A Psychological Analysis*, Methuen, 1958, p. 8.

4 See 1 above. Brookover's experiments are reported in W. B. Brookover and D. Gottlieb, *A Sociology of Education*, New York, American Book Co., 1964, pp. 423–52.

5 *Children and their Primary Schools* (Plowden), p. 277.

6 C. D. Orth, *Social Structure and the Learning Climate*, Bailey and Swinfen, 1962. See also various studies in N. Sanford, *The American College*, New York, J. Wiley, 1962.

7 P. H. Taylor, 'Children's evaluation of the good teacher', *Brit. Jrn. Ed. Psychol.*, vol. 32, 1962, pp. 258–66.

8 R. F. Bales, *Interaction Process Analysis*, Cambridge, Mass., Addison-Wesley, 1950.

9 W. Taylor, *The Secondary Modern School*, Faber and Faber, 1963.

10 S. Scheidlinger, *Psychoanalysis and Group Behavior*, New York, W. W. Norton, 1952, p. 184.

Chapter 9: The school as an organization

1 The function of culture in giving meanings to individuals was discussed in Chapter 2. See H. C. Bredemeier and R. M. Stephenson *op. cit.* (ch. 2.3) for a discussion of this. Cathectic, derived from S. Freud's idea of cathexis, refers to the way things come to be felt to be pleasant or painful. There is no common word which can be used in its place.

2 F. Musgrave and P. H. Taylor, 'Teachers' and parents' conception of the teacher's role', *Brit. Jrn. Ed. Psych.*, vol. XXXV, Part 2, 1965, pp. 171–8.

3 B. N. Sugarman, 'Social class and values as related to achievement and conduct in school', *Soc. Rev.*, vol. 14, No. 3, New Series, 1966, pp. 287–301.

4 *Children and their Primary Schools* (Plowden), pp. 203–9 and 489–93.

5 O. J. Dunlop, *English Apprenticeship and Child Labour*, Fisher Unwin, 1912. While many received a genuine apprenticeship, the term often meant going into service or employment without moral supervision.

6 J. W. Adamson, *op. cit.*, Preface. See also M. G. Jones, *The Charity School Movement*, Cambridge U.P., 1938.

7 J. Kay Shuttleworth, *Four Periods of Public Education*, London, 1862, p. 132.

8 G. A. N. Lowndes (ch. 5.20), p. 240. See also D. V. Glass, 'Education and social change', in A. H. Halsey (ch. 1.6), pp. 391–413.

9 A. B. Clegg, 'Social factors', *Education*, vol. 119, No. 3100, 22 June 1962, pp. 15–16. The description of the single West Riding school can be found in *Delinquency and Discipline, op. cit.*

10 J. B. Mays, *op. cit.*, pp. 70–3.

11 D. H. Hargreaves, *op. cit.*

12 G. A. Dell, 'Social factors and school influence in juvenile delinquency', *Brit. Jrn. Ed. Psych.*, vol. XXXII, Part 3, 1963, pp. 312–22.

13 H. T. Himmelweit, A. H. Halsey and A. N. Oppenheim, 'The views of adolescents on some aspects of social class structure', *Brit Jrn. Soc.*, vol. III, 2, 1952, pp. 148–72.

14 D. V. Glass, *Social Mobility in Britain*, Routledge and Kegan Paul, 1954, pp. 177–217.

15 J. W. B. Douglas (ch. 3.4), pp. 119–28.

16 J. H. Goldthorpe, D. Lockwood, F. Bechofer and J. Platt, 'The affluent worker and the thesis of embourgeoisement', *Sociology*, vol. 1, No. 1, 1967, pp. 11–31.

17 See A. Etzioni, *Modern Organizations, op. cit.*, pp. 20–31. See also E. Hoyle, 'Organizational analysis in the field of education', *Ed. Res.*, vol. 7, 2, Feb. 1965, pp. 97–114.

18 This section is based on G. E. Jensen, 'The school as a social system', *Ed. Res. Bull.*, vol. 33, 1954, pp. 38–46.

19 P. M. Blau and W. R. Scott, *Formal Organizations*, Routledge and Kegan Paul, 1963, pp. 116–39.

20 W. Taylor, 'Should head teachers be trained?', *Forum*, vol. 6, 1, Autumn 1963, p. 9.

Chapter 10: Conclusions

1 This emphasis occurs in 'social systems' analysis and implies a state of equilibrium. Here the existence of conflicting values and a tendency for this to result in institutionalized conflict has been stressed. These two processes occur in a school, but both include conflict as well as harmony. Contrasting values are internalized and conflicting behaviour institutionalized, alongside those on which there is agreement.

2 See P. L. Berger (ch. 3.1), pp. 110–41.
3 *Ibid.*, p. 113.
4 A full discussion of institutionalization can be found in H. M. Johnson, *Sociology*, Routledge and Kegan Paul, 1961, pp. 19–21.
5 W. Gordon (ch. 3.7), pp. 40–1.

Further reading

The list of books that follows is divided into basic material and more advanced reading. In the former category, ease of access has been considered as well as content. Wherever possible, books containing collections of articles have been selected rather than the originals. British sources have been included where available in preference to American, although in many fields only the latter exist. The aim is a basic list. Further references are in the bibliography.

General books on the sociology of education

Basic:

BLYTH, W. A. L., *English Primary Education*, Routledge and Kegan Paul, 1965.

MANNHEIM, K., and STEWART, W. A. C., *An Introduction to the Sociology of Education*, Routledge and Kegan Paul, 1962.

MUSGRAVE, P. W., *The Sociology of Education*, Methuen, 1965.

OTTAWAY, A. K. C., *Education and Society*, Routledge and Kegan Paul, 2nd edn., 1962.

More advanced:

BRIM, O., *Sociology and the Field of Education*, New York, Russell Sage Foundation, 1958.

BROOKOVER, W. B. and GOTTLIEB, D., *A Sociology of Education*, New York, American Book Co., 1964.

DURKHEIM, E., *Education and Society*, New York, Free Press, 1956.

HALSEY, A. H., FLOUD J. and ANDERSON, C. A., *Education, Economy and Society*, New York, Free Press, 1962.

STANLEY, W. O., SMITH, B. O., BENNE, K. D. and ANDERSON, A. W., *Social Foundations of Education*, New York, Holt, Rinehart and Winston, 1956.

The sociology of the school

Basic:

BLYTH, W. A. L., *English Primary Education*, Vol. 1.

DAHLKE, O. H., *Values in Culture and Classroom*, New York, Harper and Bros., 1958.

GORDON, C. W., *The Social System of the High School*, New York, Free Press, 1957.

HARGREAVES, D. H., *Social Relations in a Secondary School*, Routledge and Kegan Paul, 1967.

WALLER, W., *The Sociology of Teaching*, New York, Wiley, 1965.

More advanced:

BARKER, R. G. and GUMP, P. V., *Big School, Small School*, Stanford, California, Stanford U.P., 1964.

HOYLE, E., 'Organizational analysis in the field of education', *Ed. Res.*, vol. 7, 2, Feb. 1965, pp. 97–114.

JENSEN, G. E., 'The school as a social system', *Ed. Res. Bull.*, vol. 33, 2, Feb. 1954, pp. 38–46.

TABA, H., *School Culture*, Washington, D.C., American Council on Education, 1955.

Schools in society

Basic:

CRAFT, M., RAYNOR, J. and COHEN, L., eds., *Linking Home and School*, Longmans, 1967.

FLETCHER, R., *Human Needs and Social Order*, Michael Joseph, 1965.

GLASS, D. V., 'Education and social change in modern England', in Halsey *et al.*, *op. cit.*, pp. 391–413.

READ, M., *Children and their Fathers: Growing up among the Ngoni of Nyasaland*. New Haven Conn., Yale U.P., 1960.

SPINDLER, G., *Education and Anthropology*, Stanford, California, Stanford U.P., 1955.

STANLEY, W., *et al.*, *op. cit.*, Parts 1 and 2, pp. 13–82.

TAYLOR, W., *The Secondary Modern School*, Faber, 1963.

More advanced:

AMMAR, H., *Growing up in an Egyptian Village*, Routledge and Kegan Paul, 1965.

DRUCKER, P., *Landmarks of Tomorrow*, Heinemann, 1959.

MOORE, W. E., *The Impact of Industry*, New Jersey, Prentice-Hall, 1965.

SCHELSKY, H., 'Family and school in modern society', in Halsey *et al.*, *op. cit.*, pp. 414–20.

The culture and group life of the school

Basic:

COLEMAN, J. S., *The Adolescent Society*, New York, Free Press, 1962.

GRAMBS, J. D., and MCCLURE, L. M., *Foundations of Teaching*, New York, Holt, Rinehart and Winston, 1964.

JACKSON, B., and MARSDEN, D., *Education and the Working Class*, Routledge and Kegan Paul, 1962, especially Ch. 3, pp. 58–96.

MAYS, J. B., *Education and the Urban Child*, Liverpool U.P., 1962.

WILSON, J., *Public Schools and Private Practice*, Allen and Unwin, 1962.

More advanced:

BECKER, H. S., 'The teacher in the authority system of the public school', in A. Etzioni, *Complex Organizations*, New York, Holt, Rinehart and Winston, 1965, pp. 243–51.

FLOUD, J., 'Teaching in the affluent society', in G. Z. F. Bereday and J. A. Lauwerys, *Year Book of Education*, Evans, 1963, pp. 382–9.

LACEY, C., 'Some sociological concomitants of academic streaming in a grammar school', *Brit. Jrn. Soc.*, vol. XVII, 3, Sept. 1966, pp. 245–62.

PARSONS, T., 'The school class as a social system: Some of its functions in American society', *Harvard Educational Review*, vol. 29, 4, Fall 1959, pp. 297–318.

SUGARMAN, B. N., 'Social class and values as related to achievement and conduct in school', *Soc. Rev.*, vol. 14, 3, New Series, Nov. 1966, pp. 287–301.

WILSON, B., 'The teacher's role – a sociological analysis', *Brit. Jrn. Soc.*, vol. XIII, 1962, pp. 15–32.

All the studies of the sociology of the school in section 2 above are basic reading here also.

Schools as centres of conflict

Basic:

WALLER, W., *The Sociology of Teaching*, New York, Wiley, 1965, is an outstanding study and the following can only supplement it.

FARLEY, R., *Secondary Modern Discipline*, A. and C. Black, 1960.

GABRIEL, J., *An Analysis of the Emotional Problems of the Teacher in the Classroom*, Melbourne, F. W. Cheshire, 1957.

LYONS, G., 'Primary school', *New Society*, vol. 207, 15 Sept. 1966, pp. 395–401

WEBB, J., 'The sociology of a school', *Brit. Jrn. Soc.*, vol. 13, 1962, pp. 264–72.

More advanced:

BERNSTEIN, B., 'Social class and linguistic development: A theory of social learning', in Halsey, *et al.*, *op. cit.*, pp. 288–314.

COLEMAN, J. S., 'Academic achievement and the structure of competition', in Halsey *et al.*, *op. cit.*, pp. 367–87.

HOLLINGSHEAD, A. B., *Elmtown's Youth*, New York, Wiley, 1949.

Order, authority and the classroom

Basic:

ANDERSON, R. C., 'Learning in discussion, A resumé of the authoritarian–democratic studies', in W. W. Charters and N. L. Gage. *Readings in the Social Psychology of Education*, New York, Allyn and Bacon, 1963, pp. 153–62.

CLEGG, A. B., 'The role of the school', *Education*, 22 June 1962.

CUTTS, N. E., and MOSELEY, N., *Teaching the Disorderly Pupil*, Longmans, 1957.

FLEMING, C. M., *Teaching, A Psychological Analysis*, Methuen, 1958.

HIGHFIELD, M. E., and PINSENT, A., *A Survey of Rewards and Punishments*, Newnes, 1952.

WHITE, R. K., and LIPPITT, R., *Autocracy and Democracy*, New York, Harper, 1960.

Children and their Primary Schools (Plowden), Report of the Central Advisory Council for Education (England), H.M.S.O., 1967, pp. 185–308.

More advanced:

DELL, G. A., 'Social factors and schools influence in juvenile delinquency', *Brit. Jrn. Ed. Psych.* vol. XXXII, 3, Nov. 1963, pp. 312–22.

ETZIONI, A., *Modern Organizations*, New Jersey, Prentice-Hall, 1964.

EVANS, K. M., *Sociometry and Education*, Routledge and Kegan Paul, 1962.

KLEIN, J., *The Study of Groups*, Routledge and Kegan Paul, 1965.

NEWCOMB, T. M., 'Student peer group influence', in N. Sanford, *The American College*, New York, Wiley, 1962, pp. 469–88.

ORTH, C. D., *Social Structure and the Learning Climate*, Bailey and Swinfen, 1963.

HENRY, N. B., *The Dynamics of Instructional Groups*, Chicago, Chicago U.P., 1960.

Sociology related to the analysis of social organizations

Basic:

BERGER, P. L., *Invitation to Sociology*, Penguin, 1966.

INKELES, A., *What is Sociology?*, New Jersey, Prentice-Hall, 1965.

JOHNSON, H. M., *Sociology*, Routledge and Kegan Paul, 1961.

More advanced:

BREDEMEIER, H. C., and STEPHENSON, R. M., *The Analysis of Social Systems*, New York, Holt, Rinehart and Winston, 1962.

GOFFMAN, E., *The Presentation of Self in Everyday Life*, University of Edinburgh Social Sciences Research Centre, 1958. See also *Asylums*, New York, Anchor, 1961.

MERTON, R. K., *Social Theory and Social Structure*, Chicago, Free Press, 1957.

PARSONS, T., *The Social System*, New York, Free Press, 1951.

Index